W9-ATT-483

CULTURES OF THE WORLD
Uzbekistan

Cavendish
Square

New York

Published in 2021 by Cavendish Square Publishing, LLC
243 5th Avenue, Suite 136, New York, NY 10016
Copyright © 2021 by Cavendish Square Publishing, LLC

Third Edition

Website: cavendishsq.com

This publication represents the opinions and views of the author based on his or her personal experience, knowledge, and research. The information in this book serves as a general guide only. The author and publisher have used their best efforts in preparing this book and disclaim liability rising directly or indirectly from the use and application of this book.

All websites were available and accurate when this book was sent to press.

Library of Congress Cataloging-in-Publication Data

Names: Horning, Nicole, author. | Knowlton, MaryLee, 1946- author.
Title: Uzbekistan / Nicole Horning and MaryLee Knowlton.
Description: Third edition. | New York : Cavendish Square Publishing, 2021.
 | Series: Cultures of the world | Includes bibliographical references
 and index.
Identifiers: LCCN 2020038708 | ISBN 9781502658784 (library binding) | ISBN
 9781502658791 (ebook)
Subjects: LCSH: Uzbekistan--Juvenile literature.
Classification: LCC DK948.66 .K59 2021 | DDC 958.7--dc23
LC record available at https://lccn.loc.gov/2020038708

Writers, third edition: Nicole Horning and MaryLee Knowlton
Editor, third edition: Nicole Horning
Designer, third edition: Jessica Nevins
Picture Researcher, third edition: Jessica Nevins

PICTURE CREDITS

The photographs in this book are used with the permission of: Cover Yuta Stolyarova/Shutterstock.com; pp. 1, 78 Marc Dozier/The Image Bank/Getty Images; pp. 3, 94 Tuul & Bruno Morandi/The Image Bank/Getty Images; p. 5 SEBASTIEN BERGER/AFP via Getty Images; p. 6 PRAKASH SINGH/AFP via Getty Images; pp. 7, 19, 59, 98, 102, 105 Petr Svarc/Education Images/Universal Images Group via Getty Images; pp. 8, 96 Hermes Images/AGF/Universal Images Group via Getty Images; pp. 9, 61 Uzbek Presidency/Handout/Anadolu Agency via Getty Images; p. 10 Paul/iStock/Getty Images Plus; p. 12 Rainer Lesniewski/iStock/Getty Images Plus; p. 14 Dynamoland/iStock/Getty Images Plus; p. 15 Yulia-B/iStock/Getty Images Plus; p. 17 ecomike/iStock/Getty Images Plus; p. 20 Salvator Barki/Moment Unreleased/Getty Images; pp. 22, 25, 100 Mel Longhurst/VW Pics/Universal Images Group via Getty Images; p. 24 Sean Gallup/Getty Images; p. 26 Mansell/The LIFE Picture Collection via Getty Images; p. 28 helovi/iStock/Getty Images Plus; pp. 29, 131 Sergio Amiti/Moment/Getty Images; p. 32 MAXIM MARMUR/AFP via Getty Images; p. 34 Lukas Bischoff/iStock/Getty Images Plus; p. 40 Mikhail Svetlov/Getty Images; p. 41 VYACHESLAV OSELEDKO/AFP via Getty Images; p. 42, 53 YURI KORSUNTSEV/AFP via Getty Images; p. 44 Sabrina Gorges/picture alliance via Getty Images; p. 48 DEA/VENDELIN/De Agostini Editorial/Getty Images; p. 51 Alexander Ryumin\TASS via Getty Images; p. 52 Valery Sharifulin\TASS via Getty Images; p. 54 Planet Observer/Universal Images Group via Getty Images; pp. 58, 72, 77, 124, 128 Taylor Weidman/Bloomberg via Getty Images; p. 62 Ozbalci/iStock Editorial/Getty Images Plus; p. 64 Martin Moos/Lonely Planet Images/Getty Images Plus; pp. 65, 118, 120 Xinhua/Sadat via Getty Images; p. 66 China Photos/Getty Images; pp. 68, 70 Uriel Sinai/Getty Images; p. 73 Laski Diffusion/Contributor/Hulton Archive/Getty Images; p. 74 Jamie Marshall - Tribaleye Images/The Image Bank/Getty Images Plus; p. 75 Yves Forestier/Getty Images Entertainment/Getty Images Europe; p. 76 Jeremy Woodhouse/Photolibrary/Getty Images Plus; pp. 80, 83, 88 Bahtiyar Abdukerimov\Anadolu Agency/Getty Images; p. 82 bladerunner7/iStock Editorial/Getty Images Plus; p. 84 Keystone/Hulton Archive/Getty Images; p. 86 Yegor Aleyev\TASS via Getty Images; p. 92 Chesnot/Getty Images; pp. 99, 115 DeAgostini/Getty Images; p. 101 Chip HIRES/Gamma-Rapho via Getty Images; p. 106 Raimund Franken/ullstein bild via Getty Images; p. 108 DEA/W. BUSS/Contributor/De Agostini Editorial/Getty Images; p. 110 Visual China Group via Getty Images; p. 112 Peter Turnley/Corbis/VCG via Getty Images; p. 113 ATTA KENARE/AFP via Getty Images; p. 114 PUNIT PARANJPE/AFP via Getty Images; p. 116 Power Sport Images/Getty Images; p. 130 zazdravnaya/iStock/Getty Images Plus.

Some of the images in this book illustrate individuals who are models. The depictions do not imply actual situations or events.

CPSIA compliance information: Batch #CW21CSQ: For further information contact Cavendish Square Publishing LLC, New York, New York, at 1-877-980-4450.

Printed in the United States of America

#29.66

Find us on

CONTENTS

UZBEKISTAN TODAY

UZBEKISTAN IS A COUNTRY THAT IS ROUGHLY THE SIZE OF the U.S. state of California. Located in Central Asia, it is a landlocked country that is mostly desert. Two major rivers, the Syr Darya and Amu Darya, run through the country. At one point, the Aral Sea was a major part of Uzbekistan. The Republic of Karakalpakstan within Uzbekistan had a fishing port on the Aral Sea. However, as the rivers were diverted for agricultural practices, they no longer emptied into the Aral Sea. As a result, the Aral Sea is around 10 percent of the size it used to be, and what remains are dried salt beds. This has greatly affected Uzbekistan and its people, taking a damaging toll on their health. For example, the area of Karakalpakstan has high incidences of deadly diseases because of the dangerous pesticides saturating the area. These leftover pesticides and the dried salt from the Aral Sea blow around during windstorms and create health problems. Additionally, even though the use of dangerous pesticides ended decades ago, the soil is still saturated with them, and they get into the crops.

Islam Karimov was president of Uzbekistan until his death in 2016.

GOVERNMENT

Uzbekistan has its own government and culture. After spending many years under the control of the Soviet Union, Uzbekistan had an equally repressive president—Islam Karimov. Because of its Soviet past and Karimov's leadership, Uzbekistan became known to outsiders for having one of the most repressive governments in the world. When Karimov died in 2016 and Shavkat Mirziyoyev came to power as president, the country started to open up. Mirziyoyev recognized the government did not serve people as well as it should and instituted a series of reforms. He has worked to improve some of the country's human-rights abuses, such as forced labor and child labor. However, while the amount of people forced into working on cotton fields has been drastically reduced, it is still not completely eliminated. The use of forced labor has caused some companies to boycott cotton grown in Uzbekistan. These companies will continue to boycott the country's cotton until forced labor is completely eliminated.

TOURISM

One area that is opening up is tourism. In the past, Uzbekistan wasn't open to tourists—in fact, the borders were closed down, and the country only recently started to open them back up in 2018. One of Mirziyoyev's goals is to bring more tourists into the country. Part of this is through the Uzbekistan Film Commission that started at the end of 2018 through one of Mirziyoyev's decrees. The hope behind this decree is to increase tourism in the country and promote Uzbekistan as a location for films.

Uzbekistan is an extremely old country—people were living in the area now known as Uzbekistan around 55,000 to 70,000 years ago. There have

been many invaders who took over the area throughout the years, and there is a lot of history there, as shown by the amount of ancient architecture. The blue domes of buildings—as well as the blue and green tiles combined in intricate patterns outside palaces, mosques, and mausoleums—are alluring to many visitors. These architectural masterpieces are renowned among tourists, especially in main cities such as Samarqand, Bukhara, Tashkent, and Khiva.

Uzbekistan is known for ornate architecture such as the ceiling of this mausoleum in Khiva.

CULTURE

Uzbekistan has a population of more than 30 million people as of July 2020. It is the 45th most populous country in the world. The population is mostly Muslim, with around 88 percent of the population following Islam and the rest

of the population following other religions. The country is also fairly young, with 45 percent of the population being between 25 and 54 years old.

Because of the Silk Road's path through Uzbekistan and the exchange of ideas and food as a result of this ancient trade route, Uzbekistan has a very rich culture. Religion, family, and food are very important to Uzbekistanis. In fact, in addition to its vibrant, eye-catching architecture, Uzbekistan is becoming renowned to outsiders for its cuisine. For example, in 2018, food video blogger Mark Wiens was invited to do a food tour of Uzbekistan. His videos were a hit and were viewed more than 10 million times, with many people becoming curious about regional foods such as *plov*. Plov is served in restaurants and places called plov centers. It is one of the national dishes of Uzbekistan and is served during important ceremonies such as weddings. It's also eaten nearly every day outside of these important events.

Uzbekistan has a few important national holidays. One of the most important to citizens is September 1, which is Independence Day. It is also called Mustakillik Bayrami. This day marks Uzbekistan's independence from the Soviet Union, which actually occurred on August 31, 1991. Festivals are a part of Uzbek culture, and Independence Day is not excluded from these celebratory events. The day is generally celebrated with concerts, competitions, and fireworks. November 18 marks Flag Day, which is the date that the state flag was legalized after the country declared independence in 1991 from the Soviet Union. Constitution Day is observed on December 8 and is a celebration of the adoption of the constitution in 1992.

Shavkat Mirziyoyev became president of Uzbekistan in 2016 and immediately started making reforms.

With Mirziyoyev creating many decrees to help cultural institutions and making reforms such as the elimination of forced labor, many international observers and citizens are remaining hopeful yet cautious. After coming to power, Mirziyoyev got started on a wide-ranging reform process. These immediate reforms raised the expectations of both citizens and outside observers. However, the country is entering a crucial stage. In 2019, social and political reforms lagged, and direct criticism of Mirziyoyev is still taboo, just like it was under Karimov. This led some to wonder if faith in the government and its reforms would start to wear thin. However, at the end of 2019, a woman was elected the speaker of the senate for the first time. In 2020, the country was starting to evaluate textbooks to remove gender stereotypes to show that women do not have to be teachers; they can also be scientists or work in technology. Uzbekistan has a long, rich history, and the country is progressing beyond the repressive reputation that it had for many years.

GEOGRAPHY

Uzbekistan has a diverse landscape, including deserts, rivers, and mountain ranges.

U ZBEKISTAN IS LOCATED IN CENTRAL Asia and primarily lies between the Syr Darya to the northeast and the Amu Darya to the southwest. However, these rivers only partly form Uzbekistan's boundaries. The country shares borders with Kazakhstan, Kyrgyzstan, Tajikistan, Afghanistan, and Turkmenistan. The location of Uzbekistan means it is a landlocked country—it has no coastlines, and its borders are primarily land.

A few of Central Asia's most historically significant sites are in Uzbekistan. One of these cities, Bukhara, was a major trade and crafts center along the Silk Road, and Samarqand is one of the oldest cities in Central Asia.

Uzbekistan is around 172,742 square miles (447,400 square kilometers), which makes it slightly larger than California. Only 8,494 square miles (22,000 sq km) of Uzbekistan is covered by water, and the remaining 164,247 square miles (425,400 sq km) of Uzbekistan is land surface.

The topography, or physical layout, of Uzbekistan is diverse. The surface is 80 percent desert, which consists of flat or rolling sandy dunes. The mountains in the southeast and northeast reach 14,763 feet (4,500 meters) in elevation. The center of industry, population, and agriculture is the Fergana Valley, which is surrounded by mountain ranges.

1

The Western Tien Shan mountains are a United Nations Educational, Scientific and Cultural Organization (UNESCO) World Heritage Site. The Tien Shan mountain range is one of the largest in the world and spans over three countries: Uzbekistan, Kazakhstan, and Kyrgyzstan.

KAZAKHSTAN

ARAL SEA

Sarygamysh Lake

• Nukus

Urganch •
• Khiwa
• Turtkul

UZBEKISTAN

KAZAKHSTAN

Syr Darya

KYRGYZSTAN

• Chirchiq
■ TASHKENT
Shardara Res.
Yangiyul •
• Angren
Namangan •
Olmaliq •
Aydar Lake
Guliston •
Bekobod •
Kairakum Res.
Qo'qon •
Andijon •
Marg'ilon •
• Fergana

Syr Darya

Ghijduwon •
• Navoiy
Zeravshan
• Jizzax
Bukhara •
Kattaqo'rg'on •
• Samarqand
• Kogon
Urgut •
Dengizkul
Shahrisabz •
• Koson
• Qarshi

Amu Darya (Oxus)

TURKMENISTAN

TAJIKISTAN

Denov •

IRAN

Tirmiz •

AFGHANISTAN

PAKISTAN

Uzbekistan is a landlocked country surrounded by Kazakhstan, Kyrgyzstan, Tajikistan, Afghanistan, and Turkmenistan.

The Syr Darya intersects the Fergana Valley. It is one of Uzbekistan's three major rivers. Another is the Amu Darya. The Amu Darya used to empty into the Aral Sea. However, because of river water being diverted for agriculture, the Aral Sea has shrunk and mostly dried up, and the river no longer reaches the Aral Sea. The third major river in Uzbekistan is the Zeravshan. The Zeravshan has also lost much of its power and trickles to nothing in the desert.

THE IMPORTANCE OF OASES

An oasis is a water hole or small body of water in the midst of dry land. It helps to make the land around it fertile and helps sustain the people and animals living in its vicinity. Oases are critical to life in dry, desertlike regions and help sustain nations ecologically, economically, and socially.

For centuries, the oases of Uzbekistan have supported some of the world's oldest and most beautiful cities, including Tashkent, Samarqand, and Bukhara. Water is a precious commodity in the nation. Trickling down from the mountains and flowing through rivers on the plains, it nurtures crops and helps nourish the herds of animals that have fed and carried travelers and residents for centuries. In the past, conquerors and foreign visitors alike were drawn to the oases, which became centers for the exchange of goods and ideas. However, not all activity was good or voluntary. Because of the importance of the oases and what they offered, these bustling areas were also the targets of invaders seeking reliable sources of water. In peaceful times, these crucial areas were often bustling trade centers. Those who settled permanently near the oases supported themselves in various ways. Farmers would settle in the area and raise crops and animals, and artisans produced goods to supply the area's markets. These residents then traded their agricultural products, textiles (especially silk), ceramics, and metalware (utensils and other objects) for the products of the nomads, who stopped on their way to summer or winter pastures with meat, cheese, wool fiber, and rugs.

MOUNTAIN RANGES

Mountains surround the desert lands of Uzbekistan. The most wide-ranging mountain systems are found in the east, where the Fergana Valley is almost completely surrounded by the Tien Shan mountains of Kyrgyzstan and the Pamir Mountains of Tajikistan. Uzbekistan lies on the edge of these mountains, which within the nation's borders are mostly foothills. The highest point in the country is Adelunga Toghi at 14,112 feet (4,301 m).

The region's mountain peaks are especially important to Uzbekistan because they are the source of the rivers that flow through the country. Only about 10 percent of Uzbekistan's land can sustain crops, and most of that land is found along the plains bordering the bases of the mountains or in valleys fed by mountain streams.

TIEN SHAN MOUNTAINS

The Tien Shan mountains span across three countries and come to an end in the Tashkent region of Uzbekistan. The south and southwestern border of the mountains borders the Fergana Valley. The Western Tien Shan mountains range in altitude from 2,296 feet (700 m) to 14,773 feet (4,503 m).

This mountain system features diverse landscapes that make it a popular tourist destination. While more than 30 peaks reach nearly 3.7 miles (6 km), the mountain system also features foothills, valleys,

The Tien Shan mountain range is one of the largest in the world. The Western Tien Shan mountains come to an end in the Tashkent region, which is shown here.

lakes, gorges, and trails. The diversity of the landscape means tourists are able to get involved with different activities in the area, including skiing and hiking.

The Tien Shan mountains are also home to wild and threatened animal species. There are 61 species of mammals, 316 species of birds, and more than 20 species of fish. There are also 17 species of reptiles and 3 species of amphibians. All of these species are found just in the western region of the Tien Shan mountains. Because of this, in 2016, the Western Tien Shan mountains were inscribed on the United Nations Educational, Scientific and Cultural Organization (UNESCO) World Heritage Site List to protect the biodiversity of the area.

The mountains are also the site of almost all of Uzbekistan's forests. Walnut groves hug the lower elevations, and evergreens, spruces, junipers, and larches (a kind of pine tree) thrive in the higher reaches. Eagles and vultures called lammergeiers live in the mountains, where they feed on marmots and mouse hares.

KYZYL KUM DESERT

The Kyzyl Kum Desert in Uzbekistan covers nearly 80 percent of Uzbekistan. For the most part, the desert is a difficult place to survive in, though it blooms for a short time in the spring in a vivid display of colors. Although little vegetation can grow in the desert, the region's ultimate value is below the surface. Minerals, metals, and valuable ores lie beneath the sands of this mostly inhospitable area. The mine at Muruntau is one of the world's largest open-pit gold mines and is the fifth-deepest open-pit mine in the world.

The desert's climate is harsh. Icy winds and frost characterize the winter, and temperatures that reach nearly 100 degrees Fahrenheit (37 degress Celsius) are common in summer. No river crosses the length of the Kyzyl Kum, which is mostly made up of sand dunes stretching from one end to the other. The wind can sweep the sand off the dunes into blinding swirls.

THE GOLDEN VALLEY

The Fergana Valley is spread across three countries: Tajikistan, Kyrgyzstan, and Uzbekistan. The valley is home to nearly a third of the population of Uzbekistan. For as many as 5,000 years, it has been called the Golden Valley in recognition of its favorable climate and fertile soil. The Syr Darya, one of the major rivers of Central Asia, runs through the heart of the valley. However, like the Amu Darya, the tributaries of the Syr Darya (in the form of streams and smaller rivers) have been diverted to irrigate distant fields. Because of this, the contours and general shape of the valley have been altered over time.

Even though the valley has been altered, it is still a fertile area of almost 8,500 square miles (22,014 sq km). It supplies most of the nation's agricultural produce, including cotton, which is vital to Uzbekistan's economy. The region is also rich in gold, copper, and oil. It is the most densely populated area in Central Asia and faces problems such as organized terrorism and drug trafficking.

The Kyzyl Kum Desert covers nearly 80 percent of Uzbekistan. Vegetation such as the trees shown here are rare in the desert. The ripples in the sand are caused by continuous wind.

The Muruntau gold mine was discovered in 1958. It measures 2.2 miles (3.5 km) by 1.9 miles (3 km) with a depth of around 1,968 feet (600 m).

THE WOLF POPULATION

The degradation of the land around the Aral Sea, where rivers were diverted to support agriculture, has left hundreds of square miles of dry, salinized (containing large amounts of salt) land. It no longer supports the diverse animal life it once did, nor the vegetation needed to feed them. Strong winds sweep across salt beds that have been left exposed by the retreating and disappearing water, spreading salt even farther through the pasturelands.

In the winter months, small animals that are natural prey for wolves—mice, gophers, and rats—hibernate by burrowing deep underground. The snow and ice then form a thick layer over their tunnels, separating the rodents from the hungry wolves, which must look elsewhere for their food.

In the villages of northern Uzbekistan around the Aral Sea, wolves have reacted to the damage to their natural habitat and to the cold desert winters by preying on the sheep herds pastured in the region. In some cases, the wolves break into the sheds where the sheep are kept and even venture into the villages to attack humans. In some towns, people are afraid to go out at night in winter because there are so many wolves. In other villages, the wolves stalk the streets even in daytime. According to the International Wolf Center, as of 2020, there are about 2,000 wolves in Uzbekistan.

FOUR-SEASON CLIMATE

The four-season climate of Uzbekistan brings cool autumns, usually mild winters, rainy springs, and long, hot summers to the desert regions. Uzbekistan is generally warmer in the south and cooler in the north. In the grasslands of the eastern part of the country, summers are generally milder. In January, the average daily temperature is 21°F to 36°F (-6°C to 2°C), and in July, the range averages 79°F to 90°F (26°C to 32°C). Night temperatures are much lower than in the daytime. Variations in weather patterns, however, are not unusual. Heavier than usual rains have often damaged the cotton crops, just as colder than normal winters have altered the movements of some of the region's animals, bringing wild animals such as wolves, foxes, and jackals close to human settlements.

PLANTS AND ANIMALS

Because of its varied topography, Uzbekistan is home to a diverse range of natural habitats. The steppes still shelter the endangered saiga antelope. Roe deer, foxes, wolves, and badgers thrive in greater numbers. In the drier regions, a large lizard called the desert monitor grows up to 5.2 feet (1.6 m) in length. It shares the area with gazelles and a variety of rodents. In the Amu Darya river delta and other deltas of the nation, jackals, wild boars, and deer thrive, though pollution in these regions threatens both the animals and the plants they need to survive.

The desert regions of Uzbekistan are home to a large lizard called the desert monitor, shown here in the Kyzyl Kum Desert.

The mountains lining the eastern part of the country shelter the snow leopard, another of the nation's endangered species. Mountain goats, lynx, wild boars, wolves, brown bears, and alpine ibex (a type of wild goat) also can live safely in the mountains, where the land has been altered less than in the desert and river delta regions. Smaller animals such as badgers, porcupines, groundhogs, foxes, and jackals live in the mountains as well, though some of the animals are in danger of extinction as a result of extensive environmental damage.

The delta areas of the Fergana Valley support their own delicate balance of wildlife. They are home to many varieties of birds, including crows, seagulls, and pheasants, which often gather along the river banks. Birds of prey are found in plentiful numbers in the surrounding mountains.

COMMUNITIES

Samarqand is one of Uzbekistan's major cities. For many seasoned travelers, Samarqand evokes images of the Silk Road and the caravans of camels that once crossed the deserts, heading from China to Europe and back again. Samarqand is one of the oldest cities in Central Asia and the world. It was conquered at various times in its history by Alexander the Great, the Arab

KARABAIR HORSE

Horses have been vital to Central Asian life for centuries. Warfare in the region was conducted by mounted horsemen who formed swift and elusive cavalries, often to the surprise and dismay of invading armies of foot soldiers. The area's nomadic peoples also depended on the horse, as well as the camel, to travel and transport their belongings from one stretch of pastureland to another during their seasonal migrations.

Through the centuries, the nomads interbred their horses. The characteristic horse of Uzbekistan is the Karabair, which developed among the mountain plateaus. The Karabair's ancestors can be traced to the ancient breeds of steppe horses that the Mongols brought from northern China.

The Karabair is a medium-sized horse that has been bred in recent years for both riding and hauling. Often several of its main colors—bay (reddish brown), chestnut (brown), gray, and black—appear in combination. Its sturdy legs and strong neck make it well suited for pulling heavy loads. The Karabair is raised on farms in Navoi and Jizak, as well as Gallyaaral State Farm.

Samarqand is split into two parts—the old city and the new city. The new city was developed during the Russian Empire, which lasted from 1721 to 1917.

caliphate (kingdom), and Genghis Khan. It reached the peak of its beauty and accomplishment under Tamerlane, who made it the capital of his empire.

Samarqand's heavy industry includes the production of machine parts and other metal products. The area around Samarqand is heavily irrigated and grows much of the country's grain, tea, and orchard fruit, as well as the nation's main crop—cotton.

At its height, Samarqand was a magnificent city of palaces and gardens. Its complex water system provided most private homes with running water in medieval times, centuries before the countries of Europe could accomplish such a feat. Today, however, this system is less effective.

The International Bank for Reconstruction and Development (IBRD)/ International Development Association (IDA) lends to governments of middle-income and low-income countries. The purpose of these groups, collectively known as the World Bank, is to boost economic growth and improve living conditions. Samarqand's wastewater management is one of this group's funding projects. The Bukhara and Samarqand Sewerage Project (BSSP) is working to improve the efficiency of wastewater management and reduce environmental impact from wastewater pollution in Samarqand and Bukhara.

The city of Bukhara was once the hub of a flourishing state populated by Uzbeks since the 16th century. As a stop along the Silk Road, Bukhara was a center of trade in a variety of prized and exotic goods, including silk, spices, gems, and gold. Today, Bukhara is vital to the cotton industry, from the cotton fields that surround it to the processing plants and factories that produce textiles and rugs.

More than 140 buildings of architectural significance in Bukhara have survived for almost 1,000 years, dazzling travelers with their beauty. Many of the structures are characterized by minarets (the towers on mosques from which followers are summoned to prayer) with blue tiles. Bukhara's mosques and palaces are evidence of the many civilizations that settled there both before and after the Uzbeks.

Among the most beautiful structures in Bukhara and Samarqand are the mausoleum of Ismail Samanid—a Muslim philosopher and leader second in

The Madrasa of Ulugh Beg is a famous site in Uzbekistan.

influence only to Muhammad—and the Madrasa of Ulugh Beg, the grandson of Tamerlane.

Tashkent is the capital of Uzbekistan and a city of more than 2 million people. Tashkent was a crossroad for trade in gold, gems, spices, and horses, from as long ago as 262 BCE. Today, it is a major industrial center. Though it had been known as a city since between the first and third century BCE, Tashkent was really just a small town when it was captured by the Russians in 1865. However, as Russian domination of the area grew, foreign leaders transformed Tashkent into a large Soviet-style city over the next century. When it was designated a stop on the Trans-Caspian Railway, Tashkent became prosperous and busy. When Uzbekistan was made a Soviet republic, the Russians made it the capital. Today, Tashkent is the economic center of the region. Many rail systems, including the Trans-Caspian Railway, which still crosses all of Central Asia on the way to China, have terminals there. It is also the seat of power for the government and the military. At one time, the city's modern downtown area was home to many of Uzbekistan's Russian bureaucrats, but most of them

Broadway is a wide pedestrian street in Tashkent that is filled with cafés, teahouses, and more.

have since returned to Russia. Since the nation declared its independence, it has been home to the nation's own bureaucrats.

Though it is Uzbekistan's capital, Tashkent is a place where the pace is still slow. Many of the city's residents get around by walking. Though the streets are narrow, they are shaded by numerous trees. A wide pedestrian street called Broadway is open around the clock, and people gather at low tables to eat and drink in the cafés and teahouses.

The first American-Soviet sister city bond was established in 1973. During the Cold War, which was a period of political tension between the United States and the Soviet Union lasting from 1945 to 1990, Tashkent and Seattle, Washington, developed close ties. The cities promote humanitarian assistance and citizen diplomacy with exchanges including visits and people-to-people exchanges of teachers, schoolchildren, and more. The sister cities are committed to creating new relationships and spreading knowledge and appreciation of U.S. culture in Tashkent and Uzbek culture in the United States. Two of the symbols of this friendship are Tashkent Park in Seattle (named for Tashkent, Uzbekistan) and Babur Park in Tashkent, which has another, unofficial name: Seattle Peace Park. The main alley of the park has around 10,000 ceramic tiles lining it. The tiles were made by schoolchildren in Seattle in the 1980s. The messages on the tiles include messages of hope as well as messages favoring peace and friendship over distrust and war.

INTERNET LINKS

www.mining-technology.com/projects/muruntau-gold-mine-uzbekistan/
This page of the Mining Technology website is centered around the Muruntau gold mine and includes information on the mining complex and how the gold is removed.

whc.unesco.org/en/statesparties/uz
This is UNESCO's official site with information on places in Uzbekistan that have been added to the World Heritage List.

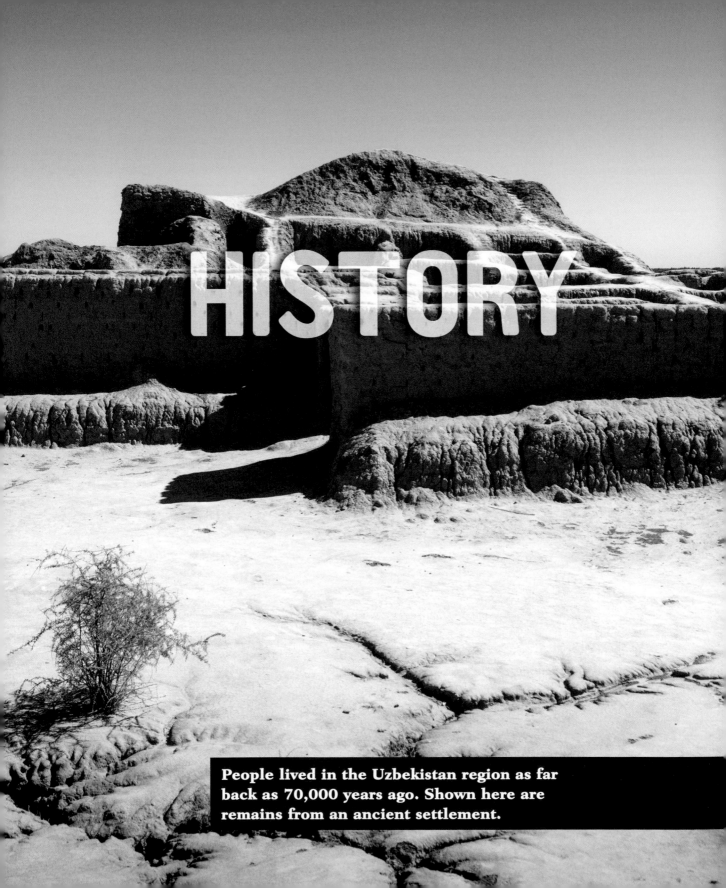

HISTORY

People lived in the Uzbekistan region as far back as 70,000 years ago. Shown here are remains from an ancient settlement.

2

PEOPLE LIVED IN WHAT IS NOW Uzbekistan as early as 55,000 to 70,000 years ago during the Paleolithic period (the Old Stone Age). In the first millennium BCE, the states of Sogdiana, Khwārezm, and Bactria emerged in the Amu Darya region. This region was later a center of trade on the Silk Road between the East and West.

Years later, in the 8th century CE, Islam was introduced into Central Asia. The religion established a foothold and spread through the region. The introduction of Islam also brought many people into the territory that was starting to form as Uzbekistan. Not only did they bring a new religion into the area, they also brought a new culture that greatly benefited the territory. While the population increased with the introduction of Islam, later invasions left behind a smaller group of people and had a lesser impact on the political and social systems. Until the Russian conquest in the late 19th century, invaders such as the Persians generally withdrew from the territory soon after they invaded it. However, these invaders still laid siege to the area. They won battles through the use of horseback archery and enslaved the people whom they allowed to live.

In the 19th century, Great Britain and Russia fought for control over Central Asia—the territory was key to the expansionist plans of both countries. After nearly 100 years of conflict, Russia succeeded in gaining control of Central Asia in 1876. Russia was in control of Uzbekistan until

Shavkat Mirziyoyev was appointed president in 2016 after the death of Islam Karimov. Mirziyoyev is shown here in 2019.

1991, when Uzbekistan declared its independence and became the Republic of Uzbekistan.

When Uzbekistan declared its independence, its first president was Islam Karimov, who was followed by Shavkat Mirziyoyev after Karimov's death in 2016. Since Mirziyoyev came to power, Uzbekistan has undergone unexpected changes, including improvement of relations with neighboring states. In 2019, the first primary elections under the new president were held, and between 2017 and 2019, around 50 political prisoners were released. Mirziyoyev has made strides toward incorporating more women into senior government positions. In December 2019, Tanila Narbaeva became the first female speaker of the senate.

TRADING ON THE SILK ROAD

The Silk Road was a series of trade routes that connected China with Europe and the Middle East. It was established in 130 BCE and was in use until 1453 CE. For the first time in the history of the area, trading rather than plundering became the main means of cultural exchange. Silk, spices, and jewels traveled on the Silk Road by caravan in relative safety. The cities of Samarqand, Khiva, Tashkent, and Bukhara—nestled in the cradle of two rivers—grew into luxurious and sophisticated centers of trade, invention, and culture. Oases and smaller towns flourished as stops on the way to the cities.

The traders along the Silk Road rarely traveled its full length. Each caravan loaded with goods traveled about 20 miles (32 km), or the average distance a camel could travel before needing food and water. When the caravan reached the camels' limit, usually at a market town or oasis, the traders exchanged their goods with another caravan that was loaded with items from the other direction. Both caravans then turned around and returned home to trade again. Traditions, stories, and music spread along the length of the Silk Road as well as goods.

Marco Polo, then a 17-year-old trader from Venice, was one of the few who traveled the whole length of the Silk Road, making his way from Italy to China in a journey with his father and uncle to the court of Kublai Khan. He journeyed

CARAVANSERAIS

Caravanserais dotted the Silk Road roughly 20 to 25 miles (32 to 40 km) apart. These were buildings that were also called guest houses or roadside inns, and they provided overnight housing to travelers along the Silk Road. Without these buildings, traveling would have been extremely difficult. Additionally, these buildings allowed for the further exchange of goods along the ancient route.

When traffic on the Silk Road increased, caravanserais were in high demand. They protected people from extreme weather and from bandits who would target caravans carrying expensive goods such as silk, spices, and more. The design of the caravanserais also reflected the fact that they were there for protection—large walls surrounded buildings, and caravans entered through a gate that would be secured with chains. Most of the caravanserais that are still in existence are now crumbling ruins.

Remains of the Raboti Malik Caravanserai, shown here, is located between Bukhara and Samarqand.

across Central Asia starting in 1271, during the height of the Mongol Empire. His route took him through Uzbekistan as he progressed north through Persia to the Amu Darya. From there, he crossed the Pamir Mountains, entering the Taklimakan Desert in present-day China. After his return, he recorded his adventures in one of the few existing written records chronicling that time and place. Much of what he wrote was news to his countrymen, and many at first did not believe him. Some scholars question if he even made it to China because of certain inaccuracies in the record of his travels and also because Asian sources do not mention him—most of what is known about him comes from his own writing.

Marco Polo's book was an early best-selling book, and it had a large impact on early explorers.

Shown here is an artist's rendering of what Genghis Khan may have looked like.

CONQUESTS OF UZBEKISTAN

The sixth through the 10th centuries CE were the years of the Islamic conquest, when Islam established a foothold and developed across Central Asia. By the end of that period, a majority of the region's inhabitants had become Muslim, belonging to the Sunni branch of the religion. The area also grew more prosperous and benefited from the accomplishments of Islamic culture. The cities of Samarqand and Bukhara became centers of learning and art as artisans, scholars, and poets established themselves in the market towns. During this time, the Uzbeks emerged as a tribal entity and began to permanently establish their presence and influence in the region they call their homeland today.

At the end of the 12th century, the Mongol tribes of Asia were divided. They were not always at war, but they generally had little loyalty to one another. Nor were they a large population, numbering around 700,000 in all. They were mostly nomadic and covered huge areas of land as they migrated to feed and shelter their animals two or more times a year. The Mongol tribes would set up yurts in the locations where they camped. Yurts are large circular tents that have an outer wool layer spread over a wooden lattice framework. The Mongols would set up camp for months at a time, usually in the same location as in the years before. Their traditional lands were in the northern and eastern parts of China until they were united by a leader called Temujin in the early 13th century. Taking the title of universal ruler, he renamed himself Genghis Khan.

Mounted on small, swift horses and free of heavy armor or any cumbersome finery, the Mongol warriors were agile and highly disciplined. They were trained in horsemanship and hunting from an early age, skills highly prized in their military society. Their weapon of choice was the bow and arrow, which they used with blinding speed, shooting accurately from moving horses. As an army, they sought territory, not wealth or loot. Their mobile way of life left them less inclined to accumulate goods than other conquering societies had been. This meant that they were more like destroyers than thieves.

As the leader of the Mongols in China, Genghis Khan united the tribes for the first time. He organized them into one army, a mobile political unit, which was still nomadic but had a government nevertheless. He allowed tribes that were loyal to him to remain as they had been and broke up those that were his enemies. He developed laws banning the kidnapping of women, which had caused much warfare among tribes, and also banned the enslavement of Mongols. He made stealing animals, or even keeping lost animals as one's own, punishable by death.

Enforcing these laws did much to eliminate the sources of strife and the causes for war that had previously divided the region's tribes. These tactics also eventually solidified his rule. Alliances with neighboring kingdoms made his reign more secure and, equally important, exposed his rather sheltered people to the cultural advancements of the rest of the world. His success in the area set the stage for him to move his influence and control beyond his Chinese boundaries.

Initially, Genghis Khan's overtures were peaceful, and he sent caravans of merchants to trade for goods for his new kingdom. When his efforts were rejected and his representatives killed, he retaliated and sent his armies westward into the land that today makes up Uzbekistan.

The armies of Genghis Khan arrived in the region outside Bukhara, having ridden across the desert in the coldest months of winter. Their plan was to frighten the inhabitants into surrendering without a fight and spare those who surrendered peaceably, forcing the men into military service. They would kill anyone who resisted. Many people took a third option and fled to the city of Bukhara. Warned of the Mongols' approach, the citizens of Bukhara threw open their gates in surrender, as did the people of Samarqand.

The Mongols, with an army of less than 200,000, went on from there to conquer Persia and Afghanistan, ultimately controlling a kingdom four times the size of Alexander the Great's. After his death at the age of 65, Genghis Khan continued to inspire his people.

Genghis Khan wanted his burial site to remain a secret. He died in 1227, and as of 2020, his tomb still has not been found. Most people interested in locating the tomb are international—Mongolians do not want the tomb to be found.

Mongol tribes would set up yurts in areas where they camped. Yurts are still used today. Shown here are modern yurts in the desert of Uzbekistan.

Genghis Khan divided his empire among his four sons, who warred among themselves and even with their own children. The region itself became less of an empire and more of a conglomeration of tribes once again. Central Asia was ripe for conquest, and the Uzbek tribes supplied a contender, Tamerlane (also known as Timur), who hoped to leave his own mark on the area.

THE RUSSIAN EMPIRE

At the beginning of the 19th century, Uzbekistan and the rest of Central Asia were key to the expansionist plans of two great colonial empires. Both Great Britain and Russia wanted to control the 2,000 unmapped miles (3,220 km) that separated India, which Britain controlled, from Russia, which could cut Britain off from its colony. The British referred to the largely unarmed conflict that

TIMUR

Timur, also called Tamerlane by the Europeans, was the last of the great nomadic warrior leaders. He was born in 1336 in Samarqand and named Timur, meaning "iron." His empire, originating in 14th-century Asia, extended from China and India to Russia.

Timur appreciated art and architecture, which led him to transform Samarqand into one of the world's most beautiful cities, filled with treasures stolen from the many lands he had conquered. Along with taking treasures, he also kidnapped artisans from the lands he won and used them to construct some of the world's most beautiful mosques, palaces, and administrative buildings. In those days of conquest, such extravagances were not paid for by his own people but from the loot of his campaigns.

However, first and foremost, Timur was a warrior, and with each conquest, his armies grew. His troops were Muslims and Christians, nomads and those permanently settled, and people of all ethnic backgrounds, including Indians, Turks, Arabs, Tajiks, and Georgians.

Timur appreciated art and architecture, and his mausoleum (a building housing a tomb or tombs) reflects that. Shown here is the entrance to his mausoleum in Samarqand.

His abilities to plan effective campaigns and to lead were unsurpassed by others during this time. His armies were always on the move, either setting off to battle or returning home with their loot.

Timur's ambition was to revive the trade routes of the Silk Road and to monopolize trade. In 1405, in what was to be his final military campaign, Timur set off for China. The ailing Timur, still in charge, was nearly 70 years old and had to be carried in a litter (a vehicle containing a bed that was carried by animals or on men's shoulders). Before he reached China, however, his illness claimed his life, and his armies turned back.

continued for nearly 100 years as the Great Game. It proved to be a contest the British would ultimately lose.

While the Russian Empire tightened its hold on Central Asia in the 20th century, it met with organized resistance from the peoples of the area the Russians would later call the Soviet Republic of Uzbekistan.

By 1924, however, a revolution in Russia had led to the creation of the Soviet Union, and the Russian Red Army had succeeded in suppressing the rebellion in Uzbekistan. For nearly 70 years, Uzbekistan was under Soviet rule. Religious practice was outlawed, and Islam was suppressed and forbidden.

As part of the Soviet Union, Uzbekistan was run from Moscow. The Soviet central planners made Uzbekistan a supplier of raw materials for the more industrialized countries and republics they also controlled. Turkmenistan and Uzbekistan became the Soviet cotton bowl. Chemicals and intensive irrigation of desert lands made huge crops of the valuable fiber possible. The development plan, unfortunately, also poisoned the land—leaving it polluted and infertile—and drained the Aral Sea and the rivers that fed it. The shortsighted planning of the Soviets left a legacy Uzbekistan still struggles with to this day. The country's strong dependence on cotton made it difficult to shift its economy in a new direction.

The Soviet government seized all private land and combined former family and tribal farms into huge collectives that they called kolkhozes. Unrealistic goals, besides causing environmentally unsound farming practices, also encouraged corruption. Government officials were offered millions of dollars in bribes to exaggerate the size of the cotton crop.

INDEPENDENCE

Uzbekistan is no longer part of the Soviet Union today, but in 1991, when the Baltic states were actively cutting the political ties that bound them to Moscow, independence seemed like an overwhelming and daunting proposition to many Central Asian states.

Uzbekistan, like the others, had never existed as a nation until the Soviet Union made it a republic. Uzbek leaders hoped that the Soviet Union would survive even after an attempted takeover in 1991 in Moscow made it apparent that the confederation was in its final days. In 1991, when the collapse of the Soviet empire was inevitable, Uzbekistan declared its independence on August 31, keeping its former governmental structure and leadership. September 1 is recognized as its National Independence Day.

The transition from Soviet republic to independent nation proved difficult. Uzbekistan had no history of self-government, nor did it have a balanced, stable economy or any established trade relations with other countries in order to obtain the products it needed. Long-repressed ethnic and religious hostilities also emerged during the transition. Though the Soviets had left the nation with a supply of well-educated and well-trained workers, the nation's industrial sector lacked the finances and organization needed to employ them.

In many towns and villages, the regular patterns that marked daily life stopped when the Soviet Union's control came to an end. Up until then, working people had salaries, industry thrived, and new facilities were being built across Uzbekistan. Many of the buildings then under construction remain half built today. Factories similarly shut down, and many have not reopened. The government subsidies that supported them have dried up, and the hope of private investment has not materialized.

In the years following independence (*mustakillik* in Uzbek), Uzbekistan formed alliances and claimed the nation had shifted to a market economy and become a constitutional democracy. In 1992, the country became a member of the United Nations (UN). Revolution Square in Tashkent became the Amir Timur Square, and a monument of Tamerlane replaced a statue of Karl Marx. The new president, Islam Karimov, was, in fact, a former communist leader who simply was given a new title. He promised to raise the standard of living and help the economy, relying on Uzbekistan's natural resources and the strong work ethic of the Uzbek people.

President Karimov announced five principles to guide the transition from Soviet republic to independent nation. First, the transition to a market economy would be gradual; second, the country would be guided by the rule of law; third, economic growth would take precedence over social reform; fourth, the government would develop and define social policy; and fifth, the government would have absolute control of all reform during the transition.

To the misfortune of most Uzbeks, the development of a market economy did not materialize. The government under President Karimov transferred ownership of a large amount of the nation's land and industries to the new state instead of private owners. Inflation soared, and investment by foreign companies proved largely elusive. Contradictory and often complex regulations as well as the necessity of bribes discouraged private investors.

Among other failed promises of reform, the rule of law was not the guiding principle in governing the people of Uzbekistan. Instead, Karimov's rule was absolute as he presided over a declining economy; a decaying political structure; a sharp rise in the number of unemployed young people; religious, political,

Islam Karimov was the first president of Uzbekistan after the country declared independence in 1991. He was president until his death in 2016.

and social repression; government corruption; increases in drug trafficking; and the emigration of intellectuals and trained workers out of the country.

Since social reform had been considered to be dependent on economic reform, social reform failed to materialize as well. Only on his fourth and fifth promises—government control of social policy and control of all reform—was the leader true to his word. Uzbekistan became one of the world's most socially and politically repressive nations in the world, with absolute governmental control. The country also had many human-rights abuses, including forced labor in the cotton fields, torture, and political prosecution.

In 2016, Karimov died, and Shavkat Mirziyoyev came to power as president. Even though Uzbekistan remains authoritarian, Mirziyoyev has worked to end some of the country's human-rights abuses through measures such as removing the ban on several websites and releasing some political prisoners. In 2019, Mirziyoyev even appointed the first female speaker of the senate, Tanila Narbaeva. As of 2020, it remains to be seen if the country will continue to improve with sustainable changes to human rights, but there is hope for change in Uzbekistan.

INTERNET LINKS

www.history.com/topics/ancient-middle-east/silk-road
This page provides information on the history of the Silk Road.

www.history.com/topics/china/genghis-khan
Learn more about Genghis Khan and his descendants.

www.nationalgeographic.org/encyclopedia/caravanserai/
This page on the *National Geographic* website provides more information on the caravanserais on the Silk Road.

GOVERNMENT

Tashkent is both the capital city and a province of Uzbekistan. An aerial view of the city is shown here.

3

N 1991, UZBEKISTAN DECLARED independence from the Soviet Union, with its National Independence Day being celebrated on September 1. After declaring independence, Islam Karimov became president in December 1991. Karimov had been involved in the government in Uzbekistan since 1989, when he became the first secretary of the Communist Party of Uzbekistan. The next year, he was elected president of the Uzbek Soviet Socialist Republic.

The parliament that was in power under the Soviet Union since 1990 also became the legislative body for newly independent Uzbekistan. Elections that were held in Uzbekistan only served to reelect Karimov and members of his party. In 1995, Karimov's presidency was extended to 2000 by a national referendum. In 2002, he was elected to yet another five-year term, which extended his presidency to 2007. The Uzbek constitution prevents a president from serving for more than two terms—much like the 22nd Amendment to the U.S. Constitution. This is to prevent any one person or branch of the government from becoming too powerful. Despite this, Karimov was elected to a third term as president in 2007 and a fourth term in 2015. Throughout this time, there were concerns about the additional terms being unfair. Even though the Uzbek constitution guaranteed free elections and declared the country to be a democracy, in reality, it was still run by the Communist Party because of Karimov's connections to that party.

The president of Uzbekistan appoints all the judges, and the legislature meets for a few days each year. The laws they pass can be vetoed, or overturned, by the president. Therefore, the legislature was unlikely to propose anything that Karimov had not already expressed his support for. Under Karimov, Uzbekistan became a repressive country with numerous human-rights abuses. When Karimov died in 2016 and Shavkat Mirziyoyev became president, there was hope for improving human rights in the country.

PROVINCES

Uzbekistan consists of 13 regions, or provinces. The provinces (called *viloyats*) are Andijan, Bukhara, Jizzakh, Fergana, Kashkadarya, Khorezm, Namangan, Navoi, Samarqand, Surkhandarya, Syr Darya, and the Republic of Karakalpakstan. The capital city, Tashkent, is also a province.

The president appoints or approves leaders of the provincial governments. They are almost always members of the political party he supports. Uzbeks elect representatives of their viloyat to serve in the legislature. They, too, must be members of the approved state party. Though they have little effect nationally as members of the legislature, their election can give them a great deal of local influence, and these positions are eagerly sought. For the most part, the legislature's representatives are Uzbeks, though other ethnic groups have elected a few representatives. The imbalance between the number of ethnic minorities and their limited representation in the government has been a cause of growing unrest and dissatisfaction.

THE REPUBLIC OF KARAKALPAKSTAN

The Republic of Karakalpakstan is a unique case among Uzbekistan's provinces. In 1990, Karakalpakstan's parliament created a declaration of state sovereignty, which is the authority of a state to govern itself. In 1993, Karakalpakstan was reincorporated into Uzbekistan. However, the Uzbek authorities would allow for a referendum on independence to occur 20 years later. This right for independence is in Article 1 of Karakalpakstan's constitution, which states that it is a sovereign republic that is part of Uzbekistan. However, as of 2020, this referendum has not taken place. Even though Karakalpakstan is part of Uzbekistan, it still has the symbols of a sovereign state, including a flag, an anthem, and a state emblem.

The capital of Karakalpakstan is Nukus, and the legislative power of Karakalpakstan is represented by the Jokargi Kenes. This is a 65-seat chamber with representatives who are elected every 5 years. Elections for this chamber took place in December 2019 with the Uzbekistan Liberal Democratic Party winning the elections. There are not unique political organizations in Karakalpakstan.

The executive power of the republic is exercised by 12 ministries, which include Housing, Finance, Economy, Health, Labor, Public Education, Preschool Education, Culture, Physical Culture, Justice, Agriculture, and Internal Affairs. These ministries each manage a specific part of the public administration and are headed by a minister.

Karakalpakstan has two supreme courts, one for civil cases and one for criminal cases, and an economic court. While it seems like Karakalpakstan is truly self-governing with a constitution, judicial system, elections, and ministries, it is a state only in name. In reality, it acts like any of the other regions of Uzbekistan. However, there are fringe groups that call for a truly self-governing, sovereign Karakalpakstan. For example, the Alga Karakalpakstan and Free Karakalpakstan National Revival Party have grown within the last 20 years and have expressed their desire for independence from the rest of Uzbekistan. However, the support for these groups is not widespread, and there seem to be no changes coming in independence for Karakalpakstan.

DEMOCRATIC PARTIES

Uzbekistan was previously governed by the People's Democratic Party, headed by Islam Karimov, the former Soviet leader. All other parties must register with the government and be approved. Registration, however, does not mean that the party is accepted. Often, a party is declared to be illegal after registration. The Islamic Movement of Uzbekistan, for example, is outlawed. Participation in an outlawed party is considered to be equivalent to committing the treasonous crime of religious fanaticism, which often results in long prison sentences. Today, Shavkat Mirziyoyev and the Liberal Democratic Party head Uzbekistan.

FREEDOM OF SPEECH AND THE MEDIA

With some governments, restrictions on opposition parties and restrictions on the press often go hand in hand. Uzbekistan has proved to be no exception, and the government considered the press itself to be an opposition party. For many years, the only people concerned with the situation were the Uzbeks. However, at the end of 2001, when the United States began its war against Afghanistan, foreign journalists descended on Tashkent as the closest safe place to cover the fighting. To their surprise, they found they were unable to acquire much information and they faced restrictions and consequences long familiar to Uzbek journalists, including imprisonment and expulsion. Many journalists left Uzbekistan under Karimov's presidency because of how they were treated. Opposing opinions were not allowed, and reporters were regularly jailed. Two journalists were jailed longer in Uzbekistan than journalists have been jailed anywhere else in the world.

Shavkat Mirziyoyev has slightly loosened media restrictions that were in place throughout Karimov's presidency. The internet had been censored for decades in Uzbekistan. Websites such as Facebook and YouTube were blocked occasionally throughout 2018, while websites such as Human Rights Watch and the BBC's Uzbek service were blocked for more than a decade. However, in spring 2019, a ban was lifted on several websites, and bloggers and others on social media are now some of the most important people influencing public opinion in the country.

Even though freedom of speech has improved under Mirziyoyev, there are still many restrictions on both the media and freedom of speech. There are also contradictions, such as Mirziyoyev encouraging the media to address important and urgent social issues although he has not held a press conference as of 2020.

INTERNATIONAL ISSUES

Though the former republics of the Soviet Union share a common history, it is not one of cooperation. After they became independent, poverty and strife in all the former republics left each too poorly equipped to contribute much to the economic well-being of the region. In addition, totalitarian regimes in Turkmenistan and Uzbekistan as well as instability in other nations have contributed to an atmosphere of suspicion. In Uzbekistan, fear of Islamic extremists left the government more likely to lay mines along its borders than to seek improved diplomatic relations with neighboring states.

Uzbekistan's diplomatic relations with Russia, however, are more cordial. Uzbekistan relies on Russia to assist it in its fight against Islamic fundamentalists and separatists of any kind. Until 2005, Uzbekistan allowed the United States to have an air base at Karshi-Khanabad, giving U.S. troops convenient access to Afghanistan, where they had been conducting a war since 2001. The Uzbek government also received Afghan prisoners that the U.S. Central Intelligence Agency (CIA) wanted for interrogation, often using methods, including torture, that were common in Uzbek jails.

National divisions between Uzbekistan and other countries proved hard for people living near Uzbekistan's borders. The arbitrary borders drawn up by the Soviets in the 20th century caused families and tribes to be divided seemingly randomly. Still, under the Soviets, people were allowed to cross the borders, and family and tribal ties were maintained. Under Karimov's presidency, the borders were closed. However, when Mirziyoyev took over in 2016, he had a few related goals: He desired a place for Uzbekistan in the international community, and he wanted to improve the country's reputation of being a closed, corrupt, and brutal place. He wanted to form a new image of Uzbekistan, improve international relations, and make up for previous mistakes. His reform work even earned the support of the UN. After decades of the borders being closed down, in March of 2018, they started to open back up.

The constitution of Uzbekistan consists of 6 sections, 26 chapters, and 128 articles.

Mirziyoyev was born in 1957 in the Jizzakh region of Uzbekistan. He graduated from the Tashkent Institute of Engineers of Irrigation and Mechanization of Agriculture in 1981. He started his career that same year as an associate professor at the institute. Then, in 1990, he was elected to Supreme Council of the republic. In 1992, he was appointed governor (hokim) of the Mirzo Ulugbek district of Tashkent. From 1996 to 2001, he was governor of Jizzakh and from 2001 to 2003, he was governor of Samarqand. In 2003, he was appointed prime minister of the Republic of Uzbekistan, a position he held until September 2016.

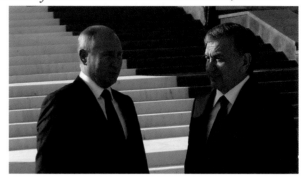

Uzbekistan has cordial relations with Russia. Russia's president, Vladimir Putin (*left*), is shown here with Shavkat Mirziyoyev.

In September 2016, he was temporarily assigned duties as the president of Uzbekistan. However, in December of that year, those duties and powers became permanent, and as of 2020, he is still president. Since becoming president, he has made positive changes that have started to improve Uzbekistan's reputation as an incredibly repressive country. He has spoken out about abuses of power and corruption and agreed that the government had not given much back to the people or served them well. He has also spoken out against forced labor, torture, and child labor. While some positive changes have been made in the country under Mirziyoyev's presidency, progress is still difficult.

HUMAN RIGHTS

In 2005, Uzbekistan's neighbor in the Fergana Valley, Kyrgyzstan, already the most democratic of the former Soviet republics in Central Asia, replaced its government with members of a more liberal party. Ukraine and Georgia also showed signs of increasing democratic leanings. Uzbekistan, by contrast, continued its crackdown on those whom Karimov called religious fanatics. After 23 businessmen in Andizhan were imprisoned for religious fanaticism, their supporters broke them out of prison, releasing other detainees in the process. At the same time, people assembled in the town center to demonstrate their support for the imprisoned men and to protest the country's poverty, lack of services, and government corruption. As the crowds swelled, government troops opened fire on the demonstrators, killing some outright and chasing down and shooting those who tried to escape. The dead included many women and children. Hundreds of people fled to the Kyrgyzstan border but found it blocked by Uzbek troops. Trapped between troops both ahead of and behind them, many more were killed.

Andizhan refugees huddle for warmth after the unrest in March 2005.

In the weeks that followed, the government maintained that 173 people were killed and that those slain were either Uzbek troops or bandits and terrorists. International human-rights workers claimed the death toll was more than 800 and included women and children. Uzbek government officials took visiting diplomats and international-aid workers on a tour of the region but denied them access to the sites of the disturbances.

In March 2020, the United Nations Human Rights Committee held a review of Uzbekistan's human-rights abuses. It was the first review since Mirziyoyev was appointed president. While Mirziyoyev has made small improvements in other areas of Uzbekistan's government, there are still many human-rights abuses that are ongoing. Some of the most persistent abuses causing a lot of concern were the use of torture, limits on basic freedoms, and keeping of political prisoners. Even though 50 political prisoners have been released since 2016, there are many more still in prison, and authorities use a section of the Violation of Prison Rules criminal code to make prison sentences longer.

Uzbekistan spent decades with its borders closed down. In March 2018, they were starting to open back up again, only to close in 2020 due to a state of emergency. In late 2019, cases of a novel coronavirus were discovered in the Wuhan, Hubei, province of China. This novel coronavirus is highly contagious. In addition, symptoms may not show up for days after a person is infected—therefore leading the person to believe they are not infected and to continue going about their daily activities while infecting more people in the process. The virus was later named COVID-19. It affected the entire world, leading to a pandemic.

When it was clear that COVID-19 was becoming a global pandemic, Uzbekistan was prepared. The first case of COVID-19 in Uzbekistan was recorded on March 15, 2020, and a week later, Uzbekistan closed its borders. Quarantine centers were set up for migrant workers who would be returning from other countries, and a special department was created to oversee the centers. However, questions arose about how prepared the country really was because a few weeks later, in the beginning of April, Uzbekistan had 172 cases of COVID-19 and the cases rose from there to 1,302 cases on April 15. By July, there were more than 10,000 cases and the borders remained closed.

Uzbekistan closed down borders during the COVID-19 pandemic. A traffic policeman is shown here checking the ID of a driver at a checkpoint during the pandemic in 2020.

Human Rights Watch expressed concerns about the border closures and citizens receiving accurate information about COVID-19. Border closure restrictions that were put in place targeted health-care workers, activists, and journalists. In addition to Kyrgyzstan and Kazakhstan, Uzbekistan threatened criminal action or opened investigations into those who spread false information about the spread of the virus. However, this also targeted doctors who were worried about having the proper protective equipment that they needed to protect themselves from getting the virus and spreading it.

One of the groups that is continuously denied human rights in Uzbekistan is the LGBTQ+ community. Multiple countries have made recommendations to Uzbekistan to improve its human rights, especially for the LGBTQ+ community, but this is one of the few issues that Uzbekistan continuously rejects recommendations on. There is significant violence and discrimination directed toward the LGBTQ+ community, and as of 2020, it is still illegal for men to identify as LGBTQ+.

Another concern of the United Nations Human Rights Committee was violence against women. Domestic violence is not criminalized in the country. Additionally, the committee expressed concerns that there was no justice for the Andizhan massacre that had occurred 15 years earlier.

INTERNET LINKS

fpc.org.uk/the-curious-case-of-the-republic-of-karakalpakstan/
This article provides an in-depth look at the Republic of Karakalpakstan.

www.hrw.org/europe/central-asia/uzbekistan#
This section of the Human Rights Watch website features articles and updates on Uzbekistan's human-rights abuses and improvements.

www.un.int/uzbekistan/uzbekistan/constitution-republic-uzbekistan
This page of the United Nations website includes the Constitution of the Republic of Uzbekistan.

www.un.int/uzbekistan/uzbekistan/country-facts
This page has information on Uzbekistan's president, political parties, and parliament.

ECONOMY

Karakul sheep, shown here, are a multipurpose breed of sheep. Their fur has unique curls, which makes it highly desired for pelts and wool.

U ZBEKISTAN IS ONE OF THE WORLD'S leading producers of cotton. Additionally, it is known for its silkworms and Karakul sheep, which are a multipurpose breed of sheep that are kept for milking, wool, pelts, and meat. Uzbekistan is also important for mineral, oil, and gas reserves. A large amount of natural gas is exported from Uzbekistan.

When Karimov ruled Uzbekistan, he never made economic reforms to the Soviet system that was in place for years. This caused the country to not only be incredibly repressed but also to struggle economically. Mirziyoyev initially was committed to continuing the previous system. However, he has changed his stance and demonstrated willingness to reform. From 2017 through 2019, the economy was growing. However, since March 2020, Uzbekistan's economic outlook has worsened due to the COVID-19 pandemic, and there is significant risk of poverty levels rising.

EMPLOYMENT IN UZBEKISTAN

Uzbekistan has a long history as a nation of traders, and its cities were once fabulously wealthy. In 1991, when the nation became independent, it had one of the more developed economies of the former Central Asian Soviet republics then emerging as new nations. Today, its economy is

4

By summer 2019, the poverty rate had substantially decreased in Uzbekistan, partially due to the expansion of small businesses.

The banking system in Uzbekistan has been largely outdated for many years, a fact President Mirziyoyev admitted during a state of the nation address in early 2020. He stated that the banks were around 10 to 15 years behind where they should be. To modernize the banks and get them to where they need to be, Mirziyoyev stated that banks with partial government ownership would be sold to strategic investors. More than 80 percent of the banking system is owned by the state, with 5 out of 30 banks being completely owned by the state. The state has a 50 percent share in 8 banks.

Historically, banks were set up to solve specific banking matters. The banks were focused on collecting cash and channeling funds into the specific sectors the banks were created for. The banking reforms that Mirziyoyev proposed were the most advanced of his reforms, and now banks are able to do normal banking business with any client.

among the weakest. In 2019, its citizens' average salary was only $235 per year (U.S. currency). This is a 31.2 percent increase over 2018. Meanwhile, the average minimum wage stands as $67 per year (U.S. currency). In a population of approximately 30 million people, 11.4 percent live below the National Poverty Line. While this figure is still high, it is a much better outlook over the 2001 figure of nearly 30 percent in 2001. Roughly 75 percent of people living in extreme poverty are residing in rural areas.

Unemployment is a major social and economic problem in Uzbekistan, and many young people leave the country to find work elsewhere. Thousands go to Russia, where they hope to find work in construction or in other fields that employ untrained manual workers. There are some areas in Uzbekistan where nearly every family has at least one relative working in Russia. Other Uzbeks find work in Korea and Kazakhstan. In some of the countries Uzbek workers emigrate to, they work illegally and are harassed by the police or the local employees they may have displaced.

Working illegally in foreign countries leaves Uzbeks at great risk of exploitation. Both men and women have been victims of human trafficking by criminals who take their passports, leaving them to work for nothing just to get their passports back so they can ultimately return home. Others are sold as commodities by Uzbek, Russian, and Kazakh enslavers.

The government controls nearly the entire labor market through a bewildering maze of regulations and laws. Security forces regularly review the books and practices of businesspeople, even the smallest shopkeepers, and impose heavy fines for any irregularities.

Under the control of the Soviet Union, production goals and labor practices were established by the central authority in Moscow. Funding created a network of grants for industries that could not maintain themselves. Since independence, not much has changed in the way economic decisions are made. Goals are still set nationally.

Most businesses supporting more than one family are state owned. In Uzbekistan, those individuals who have won the approval of the government are most able to establish businesses. This level of governmental involvement and favoritism has discouraged international investment. In 2004, Uzbekistan was considered by international observers to be one of the world's most repressive economies, an opinion that continues even as late as 2020. However, the economy is slowly starting to become more open under Mirziyoyev's reforms. Uzbekistan's main investor is Russia, whose need for natural gas supports Uzbekistan's industry.

Uzbekistan does not have what the rest of the world considers a modern banking system, leaving it a poor partner in international investment. International investors were initially drawn to Uzbekistan by its promising reserves of natural gas, oil, and gold in the early years of independence. However, its banking abnormalities, its failure to restore private ownership of industry, and its controlling and unreliable policies have caused a drop in international investment in the 21st century.

The government encourages its people to patronize Uzbekistani businesses and to buy products made in the nation, to the extent that it imposes harsh tariffs, or taxes, on imported goods. The tariffs can reach more than 100 percent, with most tariff rates falling at 20 percent. Understandably, this policy has discouraged trade from outside sources, but it has also inhibited some Uzbekistani industries that rely on parts produced outside the nation's borders.

"State-owned banks in Uzbekistan do terrible work ... I try never to go into them. You can't expect the services to be computerized. They do everything on paper, by hand. They have long lines and rude employees. Supposedly in recent years, they tried to conduct reforms, but I saw no changes. I think that privatization is the right move."
—Ozoda Nasimova, Tashkent resident

Cotton is one of Uzbekistan's main crops. Shown here are women picking cotton on one of Uzbekistan's plantations.

COTTON

Uzbekistan's largest economic sector is agriculture, and cotton is its main crop. The country is the seventh-largest producer and fifth-largest exporter of cotton in the world. The cotton is grown on government-owned plantations. Farmers are allowed to lease parts of the government plantations, but they can plant only cotton, and they are told how much they are expected to produce. Failure to meet their goals can cost them their farms.

As an export crop, cotton generates most of Uzbekistan's income from outside the country and also makes up most of its annual revenues. Since independence, Uzbekistan's government has raised the quotas for cotton production each year, though they are not often met. The quotas have resulted in systematic corruption. Farmers seeking to avoid penalties for not yielding a prescribed amount of cotton pay huge bribes to local officials who falsify the production numbers. As a cash crop, cotton has also become less profitable each year. The world price for cotton and the demand for the fiber have both dropped, as has Uzbekistan's ability to meet its production goals.

Since their days as Soviet citizens, most Uzbeks have been obliged to devote the autumn months to picking cotton. September is harvesttime, during which thousands of workers head to the fields. Schools close until December, and other industries shut down as well.

At one point, children as young as 10 or 11 worked in the fields and were supervised by teachers who were held accountable for their students' production. For up to three months each year, the children were housed in shabby barracks, farm sheds, or schoolrooms. They lived on diets of macaroni, bread, and sweet tea made with untreated water. The amount of food they received depended on how much cotton they picked. Medical treatment was either unavailable or denied, and illnesses and even deaths occurred every year at harvesttime. Often the children returned to school sick or malnourished, unable to make up the work they missed.

Uzbekistan refused to sign the international convention agreements that prohibited child labor, saying the country does not force anyone to pick cotton. Leaders claimed that everyone volunteered out of love for their homeland.

With the presidency switching from Karimov to Mirziyoyev, there were also many changes to Uzbekistan's cotton industry. First, the use of forced labor was reduced and child labor came to an end, according to a 2020 report by the International Labour Organization (ILO). Children were no longer employed to work in the fields, and 94 percent of the workers were choosing to work in the cotton fields. In 2019, around 102,000 workers in the cotton fields were there because they were forced to be, which was a 40 percent improvement over 2018.

UZBEK COTTON PLEDGE

In 2007, more than 300 companies signed the Uzbek Cotton Pledge. This pledge commits the companies that sign it to not knowingly use Uzbek cotton until the use of forced labor is completely ended. Uzbekistan is striving to get companies

GROSS DOMESTIC PRODUCT

Gross domestic product (GDP) is the monetary value of all goods and services that have been produced in an area within a certain time period. This figure includes anything produced within the country's borders. The GDP figure is used to evaluate the economic health of a country. This figure can be represented as a percentage of growth from one time period to the next.

In 2016, during Karimov's presidency, the GDP growth of Uzbekistan was 6.1 percent. It fell to 4.5 percent after Mirziyoyev came to power. However, economic growth increased in 2018 to 5.4 percent, then 5.6 percent in 2019.

to return and use their cotton again; however, this cannot happen until they prove that all forced labor has been eradicated.

In 2020, Nozim Khusanov, who is the Uzbek minister of employment and labor relations, urged the ending of the Uzbek Cotton Pledge. Khusanov pointed to the fact that significant strides have been made toward ending forced labor. However, Uzbekistan was in a difficult and unique situation around the timing of Khusanov's letter because of the COVID-19 pandemic. Because of the pandemic, the economy was severely hurt. At the time of his letter, just one month after the first confirmed case of COVID-19 in Uzbekistan, 150,000 citizens had lost their jobs; 140,000 migrant workers had returned home; and more than 200,000 additional Uzbeks fell below the poverty line. Ending the cotton pledge would improve the economy of Uzbekistan, especially during these unprecedented times. In 2001, textiles accounted for 50 percent of Uzbekistan's exports. This fell to 27 percent the year of the pledge, and in 2017, that figure was just 15 percent. However, as of August 2020, the cotton pledge was still in place.

MINING NATURAL RESOURCES

Gold, copper, and uranium are natural resources that currently play a significant role in Uzbekistan's economy. The country's gold mine in Muruntau is one of the largest open-pit gold mines in the world. Even more promising than that

are the nation's rich reserves of natural gas and oil. In 2019, exports of gas increased, and China, Russia, and Kazakhstan were the major importers. In 2020, amidst the COVID-19 pandemic, gas exports took a drastic hit. Exports to Russia stopped completely, and exports to China fell to one-third of the previous levels.

The Muruntau mine, shown here, is one of the largest in the world.

THE MARKETPLACE

The marketplace has historically been central to Uzbek life. Even under Soviet rule, the markets thrived as people continued to buy, sell, and trade their goods. Today, customs officers patrol the markets to control trade and impose taxes, but a network of exchange thrives, nonetheless, in or outside all major cities and villages.

The people employed in the nation's markets are generally a hardy group. Most have been part of merchant families for generations. In the

The Chorsu Bazaar in Tashkent is one of the marketplaces in Uzbekistan. Shown here is the inside of the bazaar with many vendors set up and selling produce, meat, and more.

country's largest market, the centuries-old marketplace outside of Tashkent, traders have at times chased the customs people out of the market. In the Fergana Valley, where unrest is apparent about other issues as well, merchants have expressed their dissatisfaction by setting fire to cars.

Traditionally, and to a large extent still to this day, the merchants have governed the marketplace themselves, making their own rules to guarantee that trading is efficient, profitable, and fair. In the past, merchants enjoyed a wide influence, because they often set the terms of contracts and guarantees and established weights and measures as well as the values of coins.

EMERGING TOURISM

The historic cities of the Silk Road—Bukhara, Khiva, and Samarqand—have attracted the interest of many international tourists. The people are hospitable, the architecture is exotic and beautiful, and those tempted by destinations that are off the beaten path are rewarded for their efforts. However, tourism is still an emerging industry in the nation, since visa requirements were strict and sometimes oppressive. As of 2020, the country is starting to slowly open up to tourism. For example. whereas ATMs would not have cash in them previously or would allow only small amounts of money to be taken out with an international card, now there are many ATMs, and international cards may be used as normal.

BECOMING AN OPEN ECONOMY

With a new president in power, Uzbekistan is making strides toward economic reforms. There are three shifts that are being made in the economy. First, the economy is switching from a command-and-control economy in which the government controls the means of production and determines the output, to a market-based economy that is run by the policy of supply and demand. The economy is also switching from being dominated by the public sector to the private sector and from an isolationist viewpoint to an open and outward-looking one. While the reform goals are ambitious and may prove to be difficult to implement in the future, the results could be that Uzbekistan becomes a more open and wealthy society.

The Hotel Uzbekistan in Tashkent was sold to a Singapore-based firm in 2020 in efforts to draw tourists and foreign investors into the area as part of the economic reforms in the country.

INTERNET LINKS

www.brookings.edu/blog/future-development/2018/12/20/how-uzbekistan-is-transforming-into-an-open-economy/
This article explains how Uzbekistan's economy is transforming.

www.heritage.org/index/country/uzbekistan?version=879
This page of the Heritage Foundation's website provides data on Uzbekistan's economic freedom as well as information about the factors that influence the economic freedom score.

www.ilo.org/ipec/Informationresources/WCMS_735873/lang--en/index.htm
This International Labour Organization (ILO) report details the use and end of child labor and forced labor in Uzbekistan's cotton fields.

www.worldbank.org/en/country/uzbekistan/publication/economic-update-summer-2019
This page of the World Bank's website provides information on the improvement of the economy under Mirziyoyev's presidency.

ENVIRONMENT

Karakalpakstan is on the Amu Darya, which is shown here in an aerial view. The river was diverted from the Aral Sea for agricultural purposes, which caused the sea to drastically shrink in size.

5

U ZBEKISTAN'S ENVIRONMENT HAS undergone a lot of contamination and abuse throughout the years. These problems have not only greatly affected the animals in the region but the citizens as well. Environmental concerns such as pollution and neglect have taken a toll on the health of inhabitants. One of the most affected areas is the Aral Sea, which has been severely depleted and reduced in size due to the diversion of water for agriculture.

By 2014, the Amu Darya stopped flowing to the Aral Sea.

ENVIRONMENTAL IMPACTS ON KARAKALPAKSTAN

The Republic of Karakalpakstan is situated on the Amu Darya in the far northwestern part of Uzbekistan, where it borders the Aral Sea. Heavily irrigated, it is a major producer of alfalfa as well as cotton, corn, rice, and jute, which is used for making rope. Other agricultural activities include breeding cattle, Karakul sheep, and silkworms. Around one-third of the population is Karakalpak, which makes up the largest group. The

Salty sediment was left behind when the Aral Sea dried up. During a 2018 windstorm, the sediment was blown around, and it withered gardens and stuck to skin.

remainder of the population is Uzbek, Kazakh, Turkmen, and Russian. The population of fewer than 2 million people is centered primarily in the delta region of the Amu Darya.

The Karakalpak people have lived near and on the delta since the 18th century. In the 19th century, citizens of the Republic of Karakalpakstan became subjects of Russia. Under the Bolsheviks, the region became part of the Kazakh Soviet Socialist Republic and was transferred as an autonomous region to the Uzbek Soviet Socialist Republic in 1936.

Karakalpakstan's 63,900 square miles (165,500 sq km) include the westernmost parts of the Kyzyl Kum Desert, where windswept sand dunes are among the landscape's few features. Rainfall is slight, and temperatures vary greatly from night to day as well as from season to season.

Almost all of Karakalpakstan's income comes from agriculture, made possible in the harsh desert conditions by the shortsighted water policies of the former Soviet Union. Throughout the second half of the 20th century, the Soviets diverted water from the rivers that drained into the Aral Sea to irrigate the desert lands of Central Asia, which were vital to the Soviet Union's cotton production.

Since independence, the former Soviet republics, including Uzbekistan, have continued to base their economies on desert-grown cotton, further draining the rivers and the Aral Sea. In addition to being severely depleted, the Aral Sea is contaminated with pesticides, chemical fertilizers, and sewage. The Aral Sea's exposed and growing salt beds have spread salt far beyond its shore, killing plant and animal life and bringing disease and death to the people of the area.

Most of the people of Karakalpakstan live along the rivers or the irrigation canals in sunbaked brick houses. The water they drink and cook with has been polluted or poisoned for more than 50 years. Some live on the shoreline of the Aral Sea, where they are exposed to even larger doses of contamination from both the land and the water.

The rates of tuberculosis, typhoid, and esophageal cancer are staggering in Karakalpakstan: Estimates put the afflicted at around two-thirds of the population. Additionally, the small region of Karakalpaskstan has a very high infant mortality rate.

> ## THE LAST CASPIAN TIGER
>
> *Karakalpak's capital city is Nukus, built by the Soviets in the 1950s as an example of what they could accomplish in the desert. What they left behind is a city of square blocks and buildings where today around 230,000 people live alongside a partially drained and polluted river. The State Museum houses the only specimens people can see of the flora and fauna made extinct by the destruction of the environment. The last Caspian tiger, also known as the Turan tiger, stuffed and mounted in 1972, watches over the collection.*

Once, the Karakalpak region was home to a diverse range of wildlife, including the Karakul desert cat, the goitered gazelle, the saiga antelope, the wild boar, the cheetah, and the Bukhara deer. Today, these animals are largely extinct or no longer inhabit this region. The only animal anyone is likely to see is the camel.

POLLUTION

Throughout the country, soil pollution endangers the lives of animals, plants, and people. Residue of DDT, a pesticide legally prohibited since the 1970s, exceeds acceptable levels by 300 to 500 percent. DDT stands for dichloro-diphenyl-trichloroethane. It was developed as a synthetic insecticide in the 1940s. It combated insect-borne human diseases such as typhus and malaria and also controlled insect populations in crops. In the 1950s and 1960s, evidence started to show how harmful the insecticide was to people and the environment. In some studies, animals that were exposed to DDT developed tumors. In 1972, the United States and Soviet Union banned the use of DDT, with other European countries banning it over the next few years. However, there are some reports that DDT was still used throughout parts of Central Asia, including Uzbekistan.

The use of pesticides such as DDT was extensive in the 1950s and 1960s, during the time that studies started to show how harmful it was. During this time, Karakalpakstan and Korezm had 78 airdromes, which are buildings that

aircraft flight operations occur at. These airdromes hosted many crop-spraying planes, which were used to spray DDT extensively over the area. Some regions of Uzbekistan were sprayed so heavily that, decades later, there are still significant health risks. Additionally, nothing was done to decontaminate the farmlands that were sprayed with DDT. The farmlands could have been taken out of use and the topsoil removed, but those actions were not taken. This means that not only are the farmers in these areas at risk because they are working in the soil, but the produce sold at markets is also affected.

Regions of Uzbekistan, such as Moynaq (*shown here*), have suffered due to the depletion of the Aral Sea. Moynaq was once a busy fishing port.

In cotton-growing areas, most of the land is polluted with chlorine magnesium. In the lands surrounding the industrial cities of Tashkent, Chirchik, Almalyk, and Bekabad, high concentrations of heavy metals pollute the soil. The province of Samarqand has pockets of arsenic and zinc contamination. Places where chemical fertilizers and pesticides are stored are especially poisoned and toxic.

Possible solutions to this heavy soil pollution include crop rotation and organic fertilizers. However, the country's heavy dependence on cotton, to the exclusion of other crops, has slowed these efforts.

BIODIVERSITY

The land and its plants, animals, and human inhabitants are threatened by many different types of environmental problems in Uzbekistan. The greatest damage has been to the plains along the steppes and the river deltas, the waters of the Aral Sea, and the nation's rivers and their tributaries. Undiminished threats come from the development of the mining industry and the use of natural areas for pastureland for animals and for growing crops. These activities have destroyed the habitats of birds and large mammals and have reduced their numbers and variety.

In a bid to preserve the country's wildlife, the government has set aside nine national parks, two provincial parks, nine provincial nature reserves, and one center for the preservation of rare animals.

SHIP GRAVEYARD IN THE DESERT

In Moynaq, there are the old remains of ships dotting the desert. This ship graveyard is evidence of one of the most catastrophic man-made environmental disasters: the depletion of the Aral Sea. Moynaq was a fishing port on the Aral Sea; however, when it started shrinking, the fishermen also followed the shrinking shoreline. When the rivers were diverted away from the sea for agriculture, the salinity levels of the sea rose, killing the fish, and ships were abandoned. Along with the salinity levels rising, the water became polluted with

When the fish in the Aral Sea died and the sea dried up, fishermen left the area, and ships were abandoned. Shown here is the ship graveyard in Moynaq, where the Aral Sea used to be.

pesticides. When the water completely dried up, salt and pesticides remained. Today, when there are windstorms, they blow around not only salt but also harmful pesticides, which is a public health problem.

The Aral Sea was once one of largest inland bodies of water—now it is less than 10 percent of its original size. Any previous attempts at reviving the Aral Sea in Uzbekistan have been abandoned; however, in 2019, the United Nations set up a fund to improve living conditions in the area. Also in 2019, residents started planting trees in the area to prevent fertile land from becoming desert, a process known as desertification. Additionally, local officials are planning educational centers in the area. It is believed the purpose of these centers is to educate students about how the Aral Sea disaster happened.

SARDOBA RESERVOIR DISASTER

The Sardoba reservoir was built between 2010 and 2017 on a canal of an old irrigation system that straddles Kazakhstan, Tajikistan, and Uzbekistan. In May 2020, after five days of severe storms, a wall of the reservoir collapsed, and water flooded villages. To prevent further pressure on the walls of the reservoir, the gates were also opened, which expanded the existing flood. The flood affected 86,486 acres (35,000 hectares) of land in Kazakhstan and Uzbekistan, killed six people, and forced the evacuation of 111,000. It is believed that building the new reservoir on top of the old system disrupted its functionality and that climate change also contributed to the disaster. Uzbekistan still uses calculations from when the country was under Soviet rule more than 30 years prior to the disaster. These calculations do not take into account changing technology or how the climate has changed since then. The building of the reservoir and the resulting disaster strained relations between Uzbekistan and Kazakhstan. First, Kazakhstan officials did not approve of the reservoir being built. Second, 32,000 residents in Kazakhstan were evacuated, and the disaster resulted in $10 million in agricultural losses in Kazakhstan. Kazakhstan has requested that the reservoir not be restored, and if it is restored, that it be reduced in size.

Shown here is some of the flooding aftermath of the Sardoba reservoir collapse, which killed six people and forced 111,000 people to evacuate their homes in May 2020.

INTERNET LINKS

www.epa.gov/ingredients-used-pesticide-products/ddt-brief-history-and-status
This page on the Environmental Protection Agency's website provides a brief history of DDT and its harmful effects on the environment.

minorityrights.org/minorities/karakalpaks/
This page of the Minority Rights Group International website provides information on the Karakalpakstan region and the environmental problems it faces.

uzbek-travel.com/about-uzbekistan/places/nukus/
This page has more information about Nukus and the environment of the region.

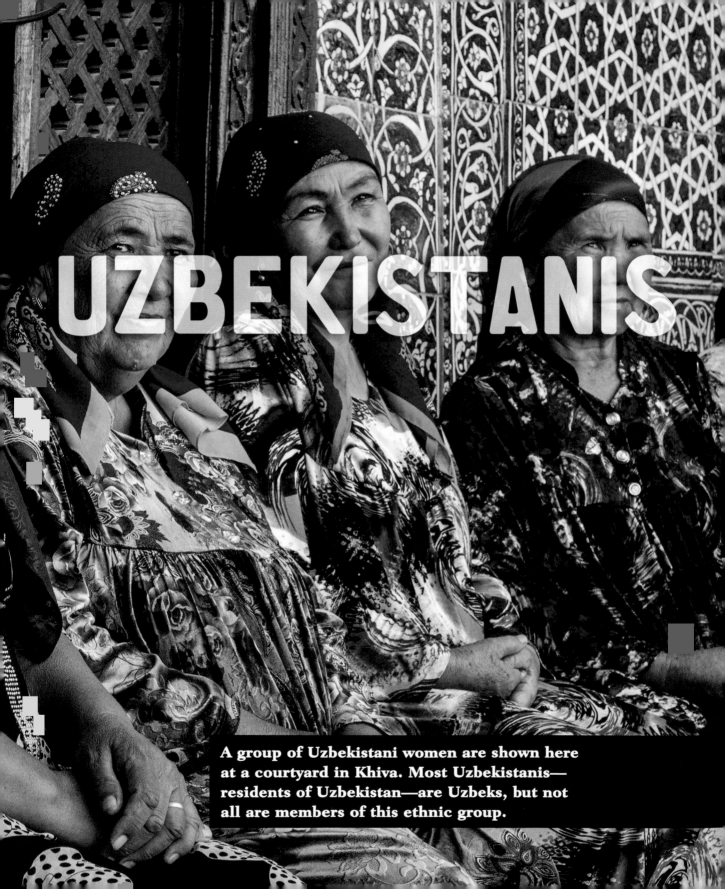

UZBEKISTANIS

A group of Uzbekistani women are shown here at a courtyard in Khiva. Most Uzbekistanis—residents of Uzbekistan—are Uzbeks, but not all are members of this ethnic group.

6

A S OF JULY 2020, THE POPULATION OF Uzbekistan is around 30 million. Most of the population is made up of Uzbeks, with around 83 percent of the population identifying as such. The rest of the population is spread out between Tajiks, Kazakhs, Russians, Karakalpaks, and Tatars. The population is fairly young—around 45 percent of the population is between the ages of 25 and 54. Meanwhile, approximately 23 percent of the population is less than 14 years old, and 16 percent of the population is 15 to 24 years old.

· · · · · · · · · · · · ·
Around 88 percent of the Uzbekistan population is Sunni Muslim.

The official national language is Uzbek, with around 74 percent of citizens speaking it. However, around 14 percent of the population speaks Russian, followed by 4 percent speaking Tajik and 7 percent speaking other languages.

THE UZBEK PEOPLE

The Uzbek people can trace their roots back to the time when they were members of the tribe of the leader Oz Beg (or Uzbek) Khan, a Mongol leader in the 14th century who brought great power to his people. The Uzbeks mingled with the Iranian peoples of the areas they conquered and with

A crowded *choyxona*, or teahouse, in Bukhara is shown here.

other Mongol and Turkic nomadic tribes during the two centuries that followed. Today, there are large populations of Uzbeks in Afghanistan, Tajikistan, and Kyrgyzstan, as well as smaller populations in China, Turkmenistan, and Kazakhstan.

Most Uzbeks are Sunni Muslims. They retain many of the traditions that guided their lives long before the Russian occupation of their lands, including early marriage, large families, and specific rituals associated with marriage and death. Even during the Soviet years, men gathered every day at the *choyxona* (or teahouse), each wearing their distinctive skullcaps. There they would sit or squat on small carpets in the shade, drinking tea with lifelong friends. Most Uzbeks kept the Uzbek language as their first language in the face of pressure from the government to speak Russian.

DISCRIMINATION OF TAJIKS

The people who are today called Tajiks occupied lands that included present-day Uzbekistan for thousands of years. The region was part of the Persian empire before the invasions of the Turkic peoples. Tajiks are the Central Asian people whose origins can be traced back the furthest. The number of Tajiks living in Uzbekistan is difficult to determine. Many have been forced to or have found it safer or more useful to register their ethnicity as Uzbek to avoid being discriminated against for jobs and government benefits. Officially, Tajiks make up around 4.8 percent of the population of Uzbekistan, living mostly in the east in the cities of Samarqand and Bukhara. Some experts, however, think that the actual percentage is around 30 percent. They think that there are possibly as many as 9 million Tajiks and that there are actually more Tajiks in Uzbekistan than there are in Tajikistan.

Tajiks are less likely than Uzbeks to go along with the state-approved form of Islam, instead following versions of the faith that were influenced by the Persian religions that preceded Islam. This, and their perceived affiliation with other countries, made them unpopular with the government of Islam Karimov, though their relations with the Uzbek people have traditionally been cordial. Before independence, Tajiks were educated in their own language, Tajik, but their schools have since been closed. In Samarqand and Bukhara libraries, books that were in the Tajik language were removed. In one Samarqand school that had 2,000 books, 90 percent of the books were in Tajik, and they were removed. Even books by foreign authors or playwrights such as William Shakespeare were removed. In addition, there were reports of books in the Tajik language being completely destroyed in 2000 because of instruction from the Ministry of Education to purge all books written before 1993 that did not follow the national ideology. In 1993, the Tajik Cultural Centre in Samarqand lost its registration status.

A dancer performs during the Nowruz festival in Tashkent.

The culture and values of the Tajiks are compatible with those of the Uzbeks and in many ways the same. They celebrate the same holidays, with somewhat different customs. For example, Tajiks celebrate Nowruz, the beginning of the agricultural year, by thoroughly cleaning their houses and whitewashing the walls. They also observe the special occasion by putting past grievances behind them, which Uzbeks do as well. Tajiks also set their tables on that day with seven things that begin with the seventh letter of the Arabic alphabet.

UIGHURS

For political reasons, some ethnic groups that have lived in Uzbekistan for centuries are not considered to exist by the government. The Uighurs are an example of people unrecognized by the nation's government.

Since Islamist terrorists attacked the United States on September 11, 2001, the Uighurs, a Turkic minority, have been identified as extremists by both China and Uzbekistan.

In 1991, the Soviet census put the number of Uighurs in Uzbekistan at 37,000. Since independence, they have not been counted, though Uighurs willing to identify themselves say the population is much larger today. Most Uighurs live in the cities of Tashkent and Andizhan.

A majority of Uighurs, however, are unwilling to identify themselves, because doing so limits their employment possibilities. Many strive to attract little attention from the Uighur Cultural Center of Uzbekistan in Tashkent,

A group of Uighurs are shown here drinking tea. The Uighurs are one of the ethnic minorities of Uzbekistan.

Etiquette, or the customary rituals of polite behavior, vary between countries around the world. Uzbekistan is proud of its traditions, and it is important for guests and travelers to follow these traditions as well.

When someone is greeting a man, it is acceptable to shake his hand. However, when someone is greeting a woman, they slightly bend their head forward. If someone is entering a house as a guest, it is important for them to take their shoes off. It is also necessary for someone to take off their shoes when entering a religious place. Additionally, things that may seem normal in some places may not fit in with the cultural traditions in Uzbekistan. For example, jewelry is common in the United States, but in Uzbekistan, it makes a person stand out. Others may think a person wearing jewelry is wealthy, so it is best to avoid displaying jewelry, cameras, and large handbags or backpacks and to carry as few valuables as possible.

which closely monitors the group's activities. Uighur life is strictly controlled in many ways, and Uighurs cannot form political or human-rights organizations.

Some Uighurs have begun to establish ties with Uighur cultural organizations in other Central Asian states. They often arrange for traveling performances and art exhibits. Others have begun teaching classes in the Uighur language, a Turkic-based language, in the hope of preserving their traditions in a hostile political climate and faced with the dominant Uzbek culture.

The average lifespan in Uzbekistan is 70 years.

JEWISH CITIZENS

Jewish people have ancient roots in Uzbekistan. In Bukhara, where the first Jewish settlement was established, local lore says they have been present in the area for more than 2,000 years. Like other groups with a long-standing history in the region, they survived the many occupations and conquests of their homeland. As in other parts of the world, Jewish people were not allowed to own land in Uzbekistan, and many became artisans and merchants. These skills served them well. Under Tamerlane, in the 14th century, Jewish dyers and weavers were instrumental in establishing the art form and the industry

behind it. Both still survive today in Uzbekistan.

After Tamerlane's death and the onset of 400 years of Islamic rule, Jewish people became second-class citizens. They were required to wear distinctive clothing and to live only in the Jewish sector. The buildings where they lived and did business had to be lower than buildings used by Muslims, and their testimony in court was not admissible against Muslims. Unpredictable and periodic pogroms (massacres) were inflicted on them throughout the centuries.

There are very few Jewish citizens remaining in Uzbekistan, and their synagogues are also closing. A prayer service at one of the remaining synagogues is shown here.

The Russian years brought a significant improvement in the lives of many Jewish people. By 1868, the Jewish population of Samarqand was more than 50,000, with 20,000 living in Bukhara. They had equal rights with their Muslim neighbors in courts of law for the first time since Tamerlane. They also were allowed to own land, and many became successful owners of factories, railroads, small businesses, cotton-producing farms, and processing plants.

With the Russian Revolution of 1917, private ownership of business and land was abolished. Free enterprise and religion were also forbidden. The number of synagogues in Samarqand fell from 30 to 1 by 1935. Jewish religious practices and identity were forced underground, as had been the pattern so often before. During World War II (1939—1945), more than 1 million Jews fled to Uzbekistan to escape the Holocaust in Europe. Some passed through the region to other lands, while many stayed and set down permanent roots.

There are two rather distinct communities of Jewish people in Uzbekistan: the Bukarim, who trace their lineage to the settlers of 2,000 years ago, and the Ashkenazi, from eastern Europe. They run summer and winter camps for Jewish children, restore ancient graveyards, and keep their synagogues in working order.

Relations between the Jewish community and the Uzbek government are relatively stable as relations go between faith-based groups and a government hostile to religion. Israel's contributions to the government's treasury help to diminish any outright hostility or discrimination. Threats come more from fundamentalist Muslim groups. For example, in 2004, a suicide bomber attacked the Israeli and U.S. embassies, killing one Uzbek guard.

As of 2019, the Jewish population in places such as Bukhara is dwindling. There are only around 200 Jewish residents in Bukhara, which is one of the places that Jewish people had largely settled in Uzbekistan. Since 1997, the number of plots in the Jewish cemetery has jumped from 9,000 to 20,000, pointing to one of the reasons why the population is so low—many of the Jewish people living in these areas are elderly, and those with younger children are moving out of the area. Since the population is so low, marrying within the Jewish faith is difficult, leaving families no choice but to move out of the area to ensure that their child is able to marry someone who is also of Jewish faith someday.

INTERNET LINKS

data.worldbank.org/indicator/SP.POP.TOTL?locations=UZ
This page of the World Bank's website has information on the population and demographic breakdown of Uzbekistan.

thediplomat.com/2016/09/the-tajik-tragedy-of-uzbekistan/
This article thoroughly examines the history of the Tajik people in Uzbekistan.

www.cia.gov/library/publications/the-world-factbook/geos/print_uz.html
This page of the *World Fact Book* website includes thorough information on the population breakdown, religion, and other information about the makeup of Uzbekistan.

LIFESTYLE

Family is important in Uzbek society. A family is shown here in Tashkent.

UZBEKISTAN HAS A VIBRANT CULTURE governed by tradition. This is seen through weddings, the use of the national headwear called *tubeteika* (skullcap), other national dress, and more. Family is also very important to people in Uzbekistan. At the state level, it is understood that family stability directly influences the welfare of the state. This is the same belief today as centuries before—religion and family are unifying and steadying influences in the lives of most people. The family system provides the order and structure around which daily life revolves.

SCHOOLING

Since independence, Uzbekistan's children have been less likely to go to school than they had been under Soviet rule, when education was a priority. Today, budgets and political priorities have left the schools with outdated and irrelevant textbooks, untrained teachers, and crumbling buildings. As of 2018, the literacy rate for people 15 to 24 years old is

In Uzbekistan, the school year begins on September 2, which is the day after its Independence Day. It ends in June.

100 percent; at 15 years and older, it is 99.99 percent; and at 65 years and older, it is 99.89 percent.

In 2018, out of nearly 2.5 million children, only 818,000 of them had access to preschool education. Preschool is important for children's physical, language, and cognitive development. It is especially important because studies show that preschool attendance greatly affects employment outcomes as an adult. However, the government has now recognized that it is important to invest in early childhood education. It has the goal of expanding early childhood education services with a goal of 100 percent of children ages 6 to 7 enrolled in school by 2021.

Along with expanding access to schools, the textbooks used in schools are also being reviewed. In February 2020, it was announced that 207 textbooks used in grades 1 through 11 would be reviewed for harmful gender stereotypes. The textbooks generally push girls toward jobs in teaching and health care instead of jobs in technology and science. Additionally, the books feature illustrations of women ironing and washing laundry. Boys are described as

Many Uzbek schools are crumbling, and some, such as the one shown here, have been abandoned.

being unable to be quiet in class, throwing stones at windows, and not caring about their possessions. The textbooks are being reviewed to remove these harmful descriptions of girls and boys.

CLOTHING

The traditional Uzbek coat, worn by both men and women, is called a *chapan*. It is a full-length, long-sleeved garment that opens down the front and flairs broadly from the armpits to the ground. Like many of the other textiles made in Central Asia, such as wall hangings and bedspreads, the chapan at its most elaborate demonstrates the skills of fine weavers and dyers. They work together to produce beautiful designs specially tailored for the garments and for the people who wear them.

The chapan is generally made of silk ikat. Ikat is a type of fabric that is produced by dying the warp threads of the fabric (the threads that run from top to bottom and are eventually tied to the loom) in elaborate patterns before they are put on the loom. The dye recipes were once the closely held secrets of the Jewish people living in the cities of Bukhara, Tashkent, and Samarqand. Weavers tied sections of the warp at precise intervals with cotton thread that would resist the dye, or prevent it from penetrating the tied-up sections of silk threads. Then, they dipped the warp threads in the dye until the parts that were not tied were the right color. When that step was complete, they unbound the threads, retied the silk warp threads, and dipped them in another color. This process was repeated until the entire warp was dyed according to the proposed pattern. Then, the warp was tied to the loom, and the weaving could begin. From beginning to end, it took a month to complete a roll of silk 544 feet (166 m) long.

Each step in preparing the ikat traditionally required a skilled craftsman. The first person was the designer, a man who carried up to 40 traditional designs

Islam Karimov is shown here putting a *chapan* on Vladimir Putin.

A man is shown here wearing a traditional black and white four-sided skullcap.

in his head. With the warp threads for the proposed fabric stretched at their full length before him, he drew on them with a stick dipped in soot, tracing the movement of the design and showing where the threads were to be tied. Next came the contribution of the *abrbandchi*, the man who tied the bunches of threads according to the design. This phase was followed by the dyer, a man who might have to work with as many as seven different dyes to get the right color for each set of threads. Working from lightest to darkest, and tying and retying the silk threads to get the proper design and combinations that would create the desired colors, he and the *abrbandchi* passed the threads between them. Once the colors were attained and set, the threads were wound on bobbins (spindles) and hung from fences and trees until they were dry. Then, the threads were unwound from the bobbins, straightened and stretched, and handed over to the weaver. The weaver tied the dyed warp threads to the top and bottom of the loom. The weaver then passed a shuttle over those threads, from side to side, weaving the cloth. When the cloth was taken off the loom, the weaver treated it with a coating of egg white and glue that he beat in with wooden hammers to strengthen the cloth and make it stain resistant.

TUBETEIKA

In the past, the shape of and the embroidery on a man's *tubeteika* (skullcap) were so individual that anyone looking at it could identify the owner's birthplace. Even today, the skullcap, brimless so the wearer can put his forehead on the floor during prayer, is part of the national dress of Uzbekistan. Though the caps are always small, they come in many shapes: four-sided, cone-shaped, round, and even shaped like a cupola (dome). The four-sided skullcap is the traditional form.

The Uzbekistan Designers Association organized a Fashion Week that was held in Tashkent in both 2017 and 2019. Fashion Week is important in the area because it helps the tourism industry and also helps with the exchange of ideas. Leading designers, experts, and other famous specialists and guests attended the Fashion Weeks. In 2017, the week started with a show on national clothing and an exhibition of national and modern fabrics of Uzbekistan. The event allows fashion houses to provide information on fashion trends while Uzbek designers gather inspiration to try to bring new elements to traditional clothing.

A young woman is shown here at a fashion show in Tashkent.

The skullcaps are always richly embroidered, some delicately, others completely covered with bright stitches.

The colors, too, are varied: sometimes a stately black and white, but more often multicolored. Flowers and geometrical shapes are the preferred designs.

FASHION TRENDS

For many years under Soviet rule, modern fashion trends were not much of a consideration among Uzbekistanis. Clothes had to be utilitarian and not call attention to the person wearing them. Since independence, Uzbek fashion designers have been exercising their long-repressed creativity to make beautiful clothing with an ethnic touch. The bright colors of Uzbekistan's past have reappeared in the silks and cottons of flowing and multilayered women's dresses. Headdresses that cover the hair, as tradition and religion often require, are bright and bejeweled as well, coordinated with the colored gowns and the long pants that women often wear beneath them. For centuries, the women of Samarqand and Bukhara set the Uzbek standard for beautiful clothing and jewelry, as the caravans carried the goods that spread their fashion influence throughout Central Asia. Today's designers hope to reestablish their lost fame with strikingly beautiful clothing that is uniquely Uzbek.

LIVING IN RURAL AREAS

Life in the country is a mixture of the modern and the old-fashioned. Four-lane highways are not only used by cars, trucks, and buses but by donkey carts as well. Shepherds on horseback keep watch over their herds of goats and sheep. In the villages, the houses are built, as they always have been, with sunbaked bricks and mud mortar. In a land with more rainfall, these building

Women are more likely to be fieldworkers. A group of women is shown here gardening.

CAMELS

The people of Uzbekistan have always had to contend with life in a desert world. Traders crossed it to sell and trade their goods, nomads traveled through it when shuttling between their summer and winter homes, warriors traversed it on their way to their next conquest, and bandits hid in it to escape their pursuers. Much of this traveling was made possible by the camel.

The camel is uniquely adapted to meet the desert's demands. To regulate its body heat in the extremes of hot days and cold nights, the camel's coat retains the skin's perspiration to keep cool during the day. It traps and holds in the body's warmth at night.

Camels are important in Uzbekistan. A man is shown here leading a camel through the gates of Bukhara.

The camel breathes more slowly and has a higher body temperature than most mammals. It eliminates very little liquid and can store a great deal of water in its body, allowing it to go for days and even weeks without drinking. A camel's food requirements are simple and minimal. It does not eat much, and what it does consume it can find for itself, generally choosing only the most nutritious parts of a plant to eat. At the same time, it is not a fussy eater and can make a meal of the saltiest desert plant.

The camel is a single-minded bearer of loads. Neither hunger nor exhaustion will distract it from what it has determined to be its job. Still, the camel is an animal to be wary of. Most owners treat it well not only because of its value, but also because they consider it to be an irritable and vindictive animal.

blocks would have dissolved long ago. However, in Uzbekistan's climate, they endure. Women are more likely to be fieldworkers than men, often using just a garden hoe to work fields that stretch to the horizon. The farms are still likely to be enormous, a system of farming left over from the old days of the Soviet collectives.

IMPORTANCE OF FAMILY

The structure of the Uzbek family reflects the country's Islamic culture. Elderly people are revered and respected, and men are considered superior to women. Generally, men and women do not eat at the same table. Especially when entertaining guests, women do not take part in the conversations with the men. Life in the cities is more liberal, and if a male guest wants his female companion to eat at the same table, the host will allow his wife to eat with them as well. When families have guests, the oldest man in the host family often says a prayer for the people gathered, expressing his hope for future cooperation and friendship. The oldest male guest then offers a prayer himself.

Weddings are a significant event in Uzbekistan. A bride and groom are shown here in Khiva.

WEDDING CEREMONIES

Without a doubt, the most significant Uzbek event is a wedding. Traditionally, brides and grooms dressed in the same type of clothing their ancestors would have worn, with elaborate headdresses and jewelry for the women and clothing embroidered with themes and colors unique to their family or tribe. Today, the wedding couple is equally likely to be dressed in Western-style bridal clothes.

Generally, a traditional Uzbek wedding lasts two days and consists of several ceremonies. One of the main events of the wedding is the bride moving from her parents' home to the groom's home. The wedding day traditions also consist of eating plov, or rice pilaf, which is cooked at the groom's home. Since family is a unifying force in Uzbeks' lives, weddings are filled with many guests, including co-workers, friends, and the bride's and groom's families.

INTERNET LINKS

uis.unesco.org/en/country/uz
UNESCO's page on Uzbekistan's education contains thorough information on school statistics.

www.uzbekistan-geneva.ch/culture-80.html
This page of the United Nations' Uzbekistan website includes information about the culture of Uzbekistan.

www.worldbank.org/en/news/feature/2018/03/16/investing-in-children-means-investing-in-uzbekistans-future
This World Bank article examines schools in Uzbekistan.

RELIGION

Muslims are shown here observing Eid al-Adha in Tashkent.

8

THE PRIMARY RELIGION IN Uzbekistan is Islam. Around 88 percent of people in Uzbekistan identify as Sunni Muslim, and they are among the most devout, or religious, Muslims in Central Asia. Eastern Orthodox Christians make up 9 percent of the population, and 3 percent of the population identifies as a different religion.

The Hanafi school of the Sunni sect gathered such prestige that its doctrines are followed by other Muslim groups.

ABOUT ISLAM

The Uzbek form of Islam follows the Hanafi school of law. Islam dates back to the time of Muhammad (570—632 CE), who proclaimed that there was only one God and that he, Muhammad, was God's prophet. Muhammad's followers, who call themselves Muslims, believe in the prophet's teachings as they are set down in his written work, called the Quran.

The faith of Islam rests on five distinct beliefs, or pillars, as they are often referred to: the first, that there is only one God (Allah), and that Muhammad is his prophet; the second, that Muslims must pray five times each day; the third, that they must fast during the holy days of Ramadan; the fourth, that they must give charity to the poor; and the fifth, that they must make a pilgrimage to Mecca in Saudi Arabia at least once in their lifetime if they can.

When Muhammad died, he did not leave clear instructions concerning who should succeed him. Thirty years later, when the matter was still

unsettled, the Islamic community broke into several sects, each with a different leader. One of these was Abu Hanifah, a disciple of Muhammad, who founded the Hanafi school of the Sunni sect. Though many Sunni Muslims believe that the four schools of law that make up the Sunni sect are equally valid, it is important to the government of Uzbekistan that Uzbeks follow the Hanafi school, which advocates that its followers obey the laws of the country in which they live.

Islam is taught in a madrasa, or school, and includes political instruction as well as the study of the Quran. Private teaching of any religion is illegal. Students are admitted to a madrasa to study only after passing an interview.

The inside of the Madrasa Tilya Kori in Samarqand is shown here.

The Hanafi school of the Sunni sect is followed in Central Asia, India, Turkey, Pakistan, and Arab countries.

RAMADAN

The third pillar of Islam is fasting during Ramadan. During the month of Ramadan, observant Muslims follow routines that have been traditional for

centuries, including fasting from sunrise to sunset. Exactly when the observance of Ramadan falls varies from year to year, and the times of sunrise and sunset vary from day to day. A card listing the hours of each day's sunrise and sunset can be bought in the bazaar. Those without a card can do the thread test: When they cannot distinguish between the colors of white and black threads held together or side by side, it is dark enough to eat.

In the hour before sunrise, families eat a large breakfast. The meal can include nuts, honey, cream, lamb, *non* (a type of bread), fruits of all kinds, and tea. For the rest of the day, they will neither eat nor drink.

After sunset, when the time for breaking the fast comes, those fasting move to the table. They say a special prayer to "open" or break the fast. Then, they share a cup of water and eat a light meal of non, tea, and maybe salad and chocolate. After a break, accompanied by more tea, women bring in large platters of more substantial foods—including meat and onions, rice, and vegetables—which will be followed by cakes or other pastries.

Religion is an important part of life for young people and adults in Uzbekistan.

Fasting is difficult, especially as the month wears on. In Uzbekistan, many families do not observe the tradition, and in many families, only some of the people do. Those who do are in the company of more than 1 billion people around the world who are fasting and meditating as they are, privately or with others.

RELIGION AND POLITICS

Under the Soviet leader Joseph Stalin, religious observances of any kind were decidedly unadvisable. Muslims in Uzbekistan were prohibited from communicating with Muslims in other countries, mosques were either destroyed or used for other purposes, and people wishing to be members of the Communist Party were required to renounce religious ties. Still, Islam was not entirely prohibited, and Islamic spiritual boards, under the direction of the government in Moscow, administered an official state form of Islam.

Joseph Stalin's rule in Russia made it difficult, if not impossible, to follow a religion in Uzbekistan, which was under Soviet rule.

This token acceptance of their culture assured Moscow of some Muslims' support during World War II. However, in the years following the conflict, the Soviet Union became increasingly harsh in its response to religious activities. Between 1910 and 1950, the number of mosques fell from 26,000 to 400 in Uzbekistan. In the 1970s, with Leonid Brezhnev in charge of the Soviet Union, the climate changed once again as he sought to expand the Soviet Union's influence in Muslim countries. Muslim leaders were encouraged to travel and to invite Muslims from other countries to conferences in Central Asia. Mosques reopened. Then, the Iranian revolution in the 1980s and the Soviets' war against Afghanistan caused a swing toward repression of Islam once again.

Under Karimov, only members of approved religions were allowed to express their beliefs or conduct religious services in Uzbekistan. People whose religions were not officially sanctioned could be arrested and imprisoned, their families harassed, and their jobs and businesses placed in jeopardy. Unapproved religions were legally considered to be a threat to the government and society. The United Nations and other human-rights groups spoke out against the repression of religious freedom in Uzbekistan. Within the country, such outspokenness was almost as dangerous as the practice of forbidden religions. Followers of forbidden religions could count on being spied on by the National Security Service, which was the post-independence version of the Soviet KGB.

Some religious organizations persevered in the face of persecution while others were banned. One of these banned groups is the Tablighi Jamaat movement, an Islamic group that emerged in the early 20th century in India with the mission of encouraging Muslims to practice their religion as it was practiced in the days of Muhammad. As of 2020, the group is still banned in Uzbekistan. In 2020, Mirziyoyev reinforced the existing ban on materials by Tablighi Jamaat. Any materials by the group cannot be produced in Uzbekistan, brought into the country from abroad, or spread throughout the country.

Separate yet related to the Tablighis is perhaps the nation's most influential unauthorized religious group. The Sufis, participants in a branch of Islam, are regarded as subversive by the government.

The greatest perceived threat to the government, however, is the Hizb ut-Tahrir organization, a group that advocates an international Islam that would unite Muslims from all countries into one state. The government of Uzbekistan considers possession of a Hizb ut-Tahrir pamphlet to be an act of terrorism, although the group does not actively promote terrorism. It draws its members mostly from populations of young, uneducated Uzbek men with traditional backgrounds. The popularity of the Hizb ut-Tahrir organization has grown as it has been forced underground and into the shadows. To its members, it is a way, sometimes the only way, for them to embrace their Islamic identity.

RELIGIOUS FREEDOM UNDER MIRZIYOYEV

Religion continues to be a sensitive subject for the government in Uzbekistan. In some ways, the country is working on improving religious freedoms along

Hijabs are an important part of some women's Muslim faith. A researcher is shown here wearing a hijab.

with the rest of the reforms Mirziyoyev is implementing. However, there are other government orders that are suppressing religious freedom. In 2019, teachers were told that students were not allowed to wear hijabs (women's head scarves), so the teachers had to make sure students removed them. The hijabs would be taken outside the school and placed in a box. This ban does not only apply to students—teachers are also not allowed to wear hijabs or other religious symbols.

There was also a beard-shaving campaign in 2019. In August of that year, police in Tashkent gathered around 100 men and shaved their beards. Then, they were photographed and interrogated before being released.

NATIONAL SECURITY SERVICE

In 2018, Mirziyoyev changed the name of this feared agency from the National Security Service to the State Security Service. In his decree with the name change, he stated the purpose of the group was to protect human rights and the freedoms of the Uzbekistani people. The purpose of the group is also to protect Uzbekistan's national interests both within the country and outside of the country and provide national security.

Mirziyoyev had previously criticized the National Security Service and dismissed security service leader General Rustam Inoyatov in January 2018. Several other high-ranking officials in the security service were also dismissed.

One of the improvements to religious freedom is allowing children to attend Muslim prayers again, which is something that was banned under Karimov. This ban was lifted in 2020, and minors are now allowed to attend Muslim prayer services if they are accompanied by their fathers, brothers, or other close relatives.

INTERNET LINKS

www.hrw.org/report/2004/03/29/creating-enemies-state/ religious-persecution-uzbekistan
This detailed report by Human Rights Watch examines religious persecution in Uzbekistan.

thediplomat.com/2019/09/religion-beards-and-uzbekistans- secular-government/
This article on *The Diplomat*'s website details the government's actions to maintain a secular government, including suppressing religious practices.

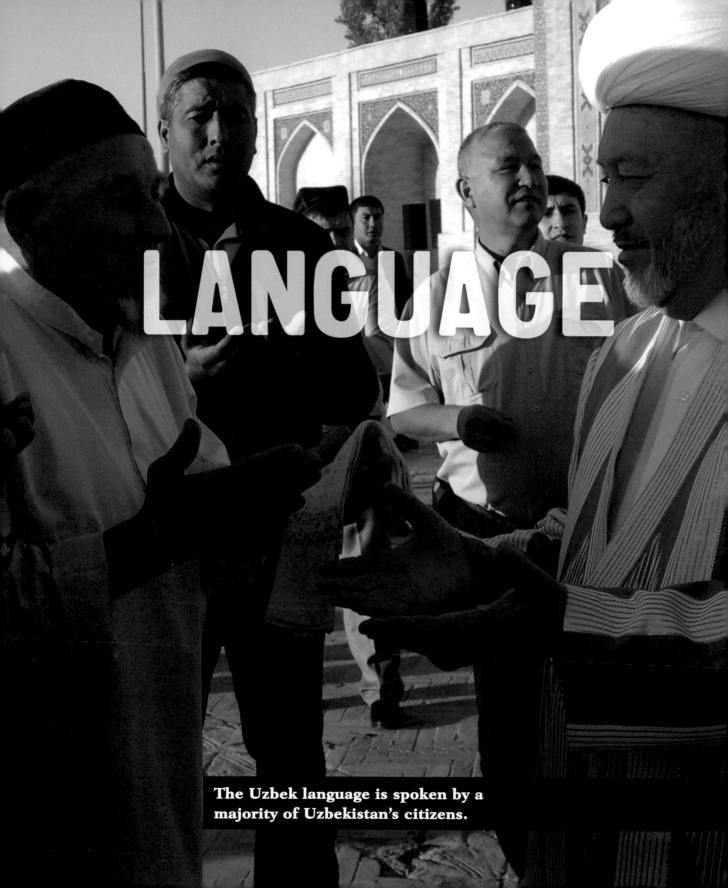

LANGUAGE

The Uzbek language is spoken by a majority of Uzbekistan's citizens.

9

THE OFFICIAL LANGUAGE OF Uzbekistan is Uzbek, which is spoken by most of the citizens living in the country. It is also spoken in areas such as Tajikistan, Turkmenistan, Kazakhstan, Afghanistan, and China. The Uzbek language has a number of dialects, but there are two main dialect groups that can be distinguished. One has influences from Iran and is spoken in Tashkent, Samarqand, and Bukhara. The other is spoken in the region of Khiva and consists of northern Uzbek dialects.

The southern dialects primarily serve as the basis for the current literary, or written, language of Uzbekistan.

UZBEK DIALECTS

It has not been easy to settle on one official version of the Uzbek language. Until the early 20th century, many scholars referred to all Turkic languages as Uzbek. Today, at least 12 dialects are recognized as Uzbek, even though their sound and word formations and their vocabularies are entirely different from one another. Linguists further distinguish between Northern Uzbek, the form spoken in Uzbekistan, and Southern Uzbek, a related but separate language spoken in northern Afghanistan.

UZBEK ALPHABET

The Uzbek alphabet is made up of 10 vowels and 25 consonants. Nouns display their case, gender, and number by suffixes added to the ends of root words. Verbs agree with their subject in case and number and show this by the addition of suffixes as well.

Today's national language of Uzbekistan has its roots in the 15th century. As in many countries that were then under Turkic rule, the people in the area that became Uzbekistan took part in a cultural movement to establish a body of literature in their own language. At the time, the dialect used had Arabic and Tajik influences, and much of the literature that has survived from that era uses words from all three languages. Today's modern Uzbek also has many words taken from Russian, especially words related to politics, modern technologies, and popular culture.

Since its first written form, Uzbek has undergone dialectal shifts based on who was ruling the country. The first official dialect approved after the Russian Revolution was from the northern part of the Uzbek-speaking area in what was then Turkistan. Today's official dialect is very different from that version and comes from the area around Tashkent.

For much of the 20th century, Russian was the language of technology and government. Education was conducted in Russian as well as Uzbek. Only the Cyrillic alphabet was considered acceptable. In 1993, a modified Latin alphabet was officially reinstated for the Uzbek language. However, as of 2019, school children still have not been given textbooks in the Latin alphabet.

Independence has brought a shift in linguistic emphasis. While Russian is still common, it has become less of a requirement for success within the country. Since few people of influence outside Uzbekistan speak Uzbek, most people striving for success make sure they speak fluent Russian—though it is not officially required. The nationalization of language has resulted in Uzbek becoming the language of instruction in schools. The effect of this has been to promote the Uzbek language despite the lack of educational resources in that language, since most schoolbooks, outdated though they are, are in Russian.

PRONUNCIATION

Uzbek is written in the Latin alphabet. The pitch of a sound also conveys its meaning when spoken out loud.

Many of the consonants are pronounced as they are in English. Some are more difficult for English speakers. The letter q, for example, is a cross between a k sound that is pronounced like a c in "cost," but pronounced farther back in the throat. Some of the consonants are combinations of letters. Two of them, sh and ch, are pronounced like the English combinations in "show" and "child." Other letters, such as z and y, are most similar respectively to the English z in "zoo" and the y in "you" but are not exactly the same. The letter g' does not have an equivalent sound in English but is similar to the gh sound in "yogurt." Similarly, the letter x does not have an equivalent in English but is like the German pronunciation of the ch in "Bach."

Other vowels are pronounced:

- a as in "bat"
- e as in "yes"
- i as in "it"
- o as in "hot"
- u as in "root"

BODY LANGUAGE

As in any culture, communication extends beyond the words people say. A glance or a gesture can convey more than words at times. The way people greet one another often reveals much about how they feel.

Men always greet one another with handshakes, even if they have not been formally introduced. They may also shake women's hands, but often only if the woman extends her hand first. Generally, men slightly bow their heads to women.

Friends and relatives of the same sex greet one another with kisses on the cheek, often several if they are very happy to meet. Women often greet one another with hugs. A younger person will often kiss an older person on each cheek as a sign of respect.

Communication extends beyond the words spoken between people. As in many cultures, body language is also important. Mirziyoyev (*right*) is shown here greeting the French president Emmanuel Macron (*left*).

In Uzbekistan and other Central Asian countries, the handshake exchanged between two men can be more than just a simple greeting. When men wish to show respect, they place their left hands over their hearts as they shake hands and ever so slightly bow their heads. This gesture can show gratitude, respect, or sorrow at parting. When a younger man makes this subtle bow to an older man, it is a sign of honor.

COMMON PHRASES

The most common greeting, known throughout Central Asia and the rest of the Muslim world, is "*assalamu alaikum*," or "Peace be with you." The person being greeted responds by saying, or "*walaikum-assalom*," or "Peace unto you also." Here are some other commonly used words and phrases:

- *iltimes*: please
- *rahmat*: thank you
- *ha*: yes
- *yöq*: no
- *velosiped*: bicycle
- *autobus*: bus
- *issik*: hot
- *sovuk*: cold
- *bazaar*: market
- *choyxona*: teahouse
- *ovqat*: food
- *kizil*: red
- *kora*: black
- *bir*: one
- *ikki*: two
- *uch*: three
- *tört*: four
- *besh*: five
- *olti*: six
- *yetti*: seven
- *sakkiz*: eight
- *tökkiz*: nine
- *ön*: ten
- *yigirma*: twenty
- *öttiz*: thirty
- *kirk*: forty
- *yuz*: one hundred
- *bir yuz bir*: one hundred one
- *bir yuz ikki*: one hundred two
- *ming*: one thousand

For centuries, most people in Uzbekistan were illiterate, but they often passed their wisdom and beliefs on to their children in the form of proverbs. Here are translations of some that have survived through many regimes:

- Shame, guilt, and disgrace are much harder to face than death.
- It is a foolish man who brays like a donkey, praising only himself.
- Words spoken with good intention are sweeter than candy.
- A wise tailor measures seven times, cuts but once.
- When they hold the sword over your head, speak the truth and fear not.

WORDS FROM OTHER CULTURES

Even before the Russians arrived, Uzbekistan's people spoke many languages and dialects. The Soviets then made Uzbek the national language and Russian the language of education and government affairs. The version of Uzbek that is spoken in the nation today incorporates, not surprisingly, a mixture of words and sometimes concepts representing and drawn from many different traditions. Some terms and phrases serve the traditions of the family, while others assume an ethnic or political dimension. What follows are words that

Uzbeks use to identify their grandmother or another older woman for whom they have respect or affection:

- *Opa* (which also means "grandmother" in German) means "older sister" in Uzbek and can refer to any older woman.
- *Babushka* means "grandmother" in Russian.
- *Buvi* is Uzbek and can refer to any elderly woman.

Other words include:

- *Eid*, or "celebration," which is an Arabic word.
- *Sovhoz*, a "collective farm," which is a word that comes from Russian.
- *Iftar*, "supper," or a meal to break a period of fasting, which is derived from Arabic.

TAJIK LANGUAGE

Uzbekistan's other main language is Tajik, which is widely spoken in Samarqand, Bukhara, and other regions in the east of the country that border Tajikistan.

A *piala* is a teacup, or small bowl that does not have handles. Two men are shown here drinking tea from pialas.

When the borders were set, the Tajik population was arbitrarily split between the two countries. Nearly 1 million Uzbeks speak Tajik. Like Uzbek, it has many of the same sounds as English, and meaning is partly determined by intonation or pitch. The vocabulary is very different from Uzbek, though.

FINES FOR OTHER LANGUAGES

In May 2020, the Ministry of Justice in Uzbekistan proposed a legal change to the language that brought a lot of criticism from the Russian media. The proposed legal change was to use only the Uzbek language in written business communications. Those who do not adhere to this will face fines. The Russian media criticized the move, stating it discriminated against the Russian-speaking population of Uzbekistan.

INTERNET LINKS

www.britannica.com/topic/Uzbek-language
This page of the *Britannica* website includes information on the development of the Uzbek language.

thediplomat.com/2020/05/can-uzbekistan-put-the-uzbek-language-first/
This article on *The Diplomat*'s website examines the controversy surrounding the government's decision to fine people who do not use the Uzbek language in official communications.

ARTS

Art plays a large role in Uzbekistan's cultural heritage. This mosaic with an intricate design is located in Khiva.

THE INDUSTRIAL REVOLUTION began in the 18th century and affected life in North America and Europe. It permanently changed the way of life for many people with inventions such as the cotton gin and developments such as the transcontinental railroad and electricity. In Central Asia, especially in Uzbekistan, however, people continued to make goods as they previously had. They made items one at a time using traditions passed down from father to son and mother to daughter. These traditions are seen in items such as jewelry, woodwork, and more. Crafts and arts play a large role in the cultural heritage of Uzbekistan.

SOVIET-ERA CRAFTS

The traditions of craftspeople go back hundreds of years in Uzbekistan, to when daily life and practice determined the type and decoration of the articles. These styles, techniques, and forms were passed down from

10

Tashkent's 29 subway stations are filled with elaborate mosaics and chandeliers.

one generation to the next. The Russian domination of Uzbekistan in the 20th century had two rather contradictory effects on Uzbek craftsmanship. On the one hand, Soviet ideology severely restricted both the types and the decorations of articles. For example, the Soviet rulers declared that traditionally decorated wooden cradles and wedding gowns embroidered with golden threads were leftovers of a feudal state of mind, so they banned them from both use and production. In addition, they ordered that decorative themes and subjects should glorify the Soviet state and ideology. This drastically changed the appearance, if not the techniques, of articles produced under their rule.

On the other hand, in their attempt to document social history, the Soviets sent scientists and ethnographers into the cities and rural areas to record the traditional methods and designs of the artisans. As part of their study, the scholars collected and catalogued many of the artifacts they found. Though many pre-Soviet paintings and works of literature were considered

The subway stations in Tashkent feature elaborate artwork that had not been seen by outsiders until a photography ban was lifted in 2017. One of the interior decorations in the station is shown here.

unacceptable in content and intention and were destroyed, most practical and household items were preserved, even if the particular object was considered an example of what the Soviets believed needed to be replaced.

The result of these two often contradictory impulses—one to control artisans and their crafts and the other to record their techniques and traditions—was that, though production suffered in terms of artistic quality and variety, the pre-Soviet arts were well documented and preserved in museums and libraries. Since independence, traditional themes have been revived as a reflection of national pride. The records and collections of the Soviets have at times been sources of knowledge for this revival. Because the Soviet policies restricted the output and free expression of artisans, traditions were lost or suppressed for several generations. Today, craftspeople can reintroduce and embrace the styles and patterns that are central to Uzbek culture but were once threatened with extinction.

Coral and silver jewelry from Bukhara is shown here.

JEWELERS

Jewelry making, like all of Uzbekistan's arts, follows a long-standing tradition interrupted in the 20th century by Soviet restrictions on materials and requirements for conformity. From the 19th century, jewelers, known as *zargars*, worked with precious metals and stones to create beautiful ornaments that had spiritual significance.

Today, jewelers are once again allowed to work with precious metals, and many silversmiths are reviving traditional designs. Until recently, traditional jewelry pieces were kept locked away as family treasures or could only be seen in museums.

The *tumar*, an ancient form of jewelry, is a small container that comes in many shapes and is used to keep a charm or a bit of paper with a prayer written on it. Throughout Central Asia, people wear these charms in the hope that their fortunes will prosper. In Bukhara, the tumar is tube shaped with silver filigree (ornate) work and blue stones the color of the domes of Samarqand. Delicate balls, hanging from a crescent shape on fine chains, transform the basic tumar into earrings or pendants.

WOODWORKERS

The art of carving and painting wood has roots in the Uzbek architecture of the Middle Ages. In the city markets, craftspeople sell intricately carved and painted six-sided tables; low stools that suit yurts and teahouses better than chairs do; book stands, used most often in Uzbekistan to hold and display the Quran; and pencil boxes for tourists.

Wood-carvers have often been key to the development and practice of the arts in other fields. Musicians, weavers, chess masters, and horseback riders use musical instruments, stamps for making printed fabrics, chess sets, and even saddles and carts that the woodworkers have made.

Woodworkers can create detailed works of art out of wood, such as these doors at the Dorut Tilovat Complex in Shakhrisabz.

Trees are not plentiful in Uzbekistan, but they are varied. Woodworkers use plane, elm, walnut, mulberry, juniper, poplar, pear, and quince. Always working with the texture and pattern of the wood, craftspeople ornament their work with carvings, paintings, and inlays of other woods. Many of today's artisans, who are regaining respect for the craft that was lost during the Soviet years, specialize in using particular woods.

Khiva is one of the oldest centers for wood carving in Central Asia. While most of the artisans in Uzbekistan specialize in one particular type of woodworking, the workers of Khiva have traditionally been masters of all. Each Khivan master is a carpenter, joiner, carver, engraver, and turner. He starts with trees and blocks of wood and ends up with a finished product. Khivan woodworkers are famous for their wooden trellises, musical instruments, and carved doors and pillars. Much of what they built in the 19th century still exists, particularly doors made of apricot and mulberry wood that are used in many Khivan houses.

FORBIDDEN ART

For years, sandstorms spread polluted soil and air through the streets of Nukus, a place that was a small development in the 1930s that transformed when the Soviets built a city there in 1950 to show what they could accomplish in the desert. There, amid square concrete buildings arranged in square concrete blocks, the people have managed to do something that eluded artists and collectors throughout the rest of the

Igor Savitsy preserved many paintings, including those shown here at the Nukus Museum of Art.

Soviet Union: preserve the art targeted by Stalinist purges in the 1930s, when millions of people were murdered and all traces of their artistic traditions were erased. In one of Earth's most desolate places, the Nukus Museum of Art preserves a collection of cubist, surrealist, and Western-style paintings and landscapes by artists who were murdered or who disappeared into the Soviet labor camps. Artist and scholar Igor Savitsky, helped by Nukus's isolation, managed to preserve a collection of more than 80,000 paintings.

FABRIC

Since the days of the Silk Road, Samarqand, Bukhara, Kokand, and Tashkent have been famous for their markets filled with woven, embroidered, and felted cloth. Silk was especially in demand on the western end of the trade route. The Fergana Valley was an early producer of silk, cotton, and printed fabrics.

Suzani fabric is shown here for sale at a market in Bukhara.

Today, much of the cloth sold abroad and to tourists is made in large factories that were established by the Soviets.

Uzbekistan's most characteristic fabric is the *suzani*, named for the Persian word for "needle." A suzani is a cotton or silk cloth embroidered with brightly colored silk threads that form dazzling designs such as pomegranates, flowers, moons, and shapes with jagged points that are believed to protect the wearer or viewer from evil. Traditionally, sewing suzanis was the only way for women to participate in the visual arts. They worked their elaborate designs in tiny chainstitches that covered the cloth with an overall design of beauty as well as symbolic power. Suzanis—in the form of bedspreads, wall hangings, and clothing—were part of every young woman's dowry, or the wealth that she brought to her husband in marriage.

Weaving has been part of life in Uzbekistan for centuries. Nomadic women spun the wool from their sheep, dyed it in natural colors extracted from the plants they grew or gathered, and wove everything their family needed on looms that they staked out in the ground or in their yurt. Bags, covers, blankets, rugs, and hangings all had specific uses and were woven to the size and shape that best served their particular purpose. Designs and techniques were handed down through the generations, and young girls learned early how to prepare the wool and attach the warp threads to the loom.

Travelers and collectors have long treasured tribal rugs that are made in Uzbekistan. The most famous, the Bukhara, is a repeating pattern of guls, or eight-sided shapes. It was named after the city where it was sold to travelers, even though this dark red carpet was often woven by nomadic Turkmens and not actually made in Bukhara.

In addition to Bukhara, Tashkent and Samarqand were also important centers of weaving. In the 20th century, the Soviet planners forced many of the weavers to work together in large factories, and the quality and variety

Dilyara Kaipova is a textile artist with interests in embroidery, needlework, and knitting. Her first textile project was called "Captain Ikat." Her goal was to explore how a traditional art, such as ikat fabric, could be devalued and absorbed by symbols of mass culture. As a result, she created ikat fabric with a pop culture twist. Popular symbols such as Captain America's shield, Darth Vader's mask, Mickey Mouse, the Batman symbol, aliens, and more were woven into her fabrics.

Her process uses centuries-old techniques and natural dyes and results in a finished cloth that is around 721 feet (220 m) long. The fabric is used for scarves, chapans, and more. Kaipova's work has been featured in exhibitions in Tashkent in 2016, the National Gallery of Uzbekistan in 2017, and the Aspan Gallery in Almaty, Kazakhstan, in 2020.

of products declined. Today, there are artisan weavers in Uzbekistan, but the ordinary day-to-day weaving performed by women has become less common.

Silk production—from mulberry tree to silkworm to finished cloth—has long been an esteemed artisan's skill in Uzbekistan. Gold embroidery, too, has been a feature of the finest cloth since at least the 14th century, though it has been found in tombs dating back 1,200 years before that time. Special silk household items and women's clothing were generally decorated mainly with plant designs. Unlike suzani embroiderers, the gold embroiderers were men. Under the communists, though, women's clothes were dropped from the gold embroiderers' repertoire, declared to be unnecessary finery. The men were organized into large workshops where they were ordered to produce specific items. The real gold of traditional embroideries was replaced with rayon, and the art has since disappeared.

UZBEK WRITERS

In the Middle Ages, the cities of Uzbekistan were renowned centers of learning. The Muslim world celebrated its scholars and encouraged their inquiries and investigations. Many scientists and philosophers prospered, and their discoveries in medicine and science predated many of the developments made in the West. Many of the scholars were poets and philosophers as well.

Mir Ali Shir Nava'i is considered to be the father of Uzbek literature. His writings in Chagatai, the linguistic predecessor of Uzbek, showed how beautifully his native language could be used for the creation of poetry. Though he was born and died in Herat, he spent most of his life in Samarqand, where he used his wealth to endow mosques, schools, and hospitals. His poetry included romances that recounted the legends of his people and poems with a strongly philosophical turn encouraging hard work, social justice, and community.

Shermuhammad Munis was another scholar and poet who is celebrated for his writings in the Uzbek language. His main work was a history of events, as he knew them, from antiquity to the present day, which for him was 1813. He also wrote an epic poem, known as a *devan*, that contained 8,500 verses.

The period from the second half of the 19th century to the beginning of the 20th century was an important time for literature in Uzbekistan. Lyric poetry was the literary form of choice, and many verses were written with the intention of setting them to music. Poets were highly esteemed, and many men combined poetry with careers in medicine, politics, and science. Singers memorized poets' works, and the best singers knew thousands of lyrics.

Contemporary Uzbek writers include Shukur Holmirzaev and Sharof Boshbekov, both novelists and story writers, and Abdulla Oripov. Oripov was a literary translator, poet, and politician, and he also wrote the lyrics to Uzbekistan's state anthem. Oripov was a household name in Uzbekistan, and his works have been taught in schools. From 1971 to 2009, he was a member of the Writers' Union of Uzbekistan and served as president of the organization starting in 1994. He won numerous awards, including the State Hamza Prize in 1989, the National Poet of Uzbek award in 1989, the Alisher Novoiy State Prize in 1992, and the Hero of Uzbekistan award. The Hero of Uzbekistan Award is a prestigious award, the highest a civilian can receive. Oripov was even a member of the legislature in Uzbekistan from 2005 until his death in 2016.

UZBEK ARCHITECTURE AND CERAMIC WORK

At one time, the people of Central Asia lived in houses made mostly of sunbaked bricks. Their pots also were made of sunbaked mud, unfired and unglazed, though sometimes richly engraved. Eventually, the ceramic arts progressed.

Today, the palaces and mosques of Uzbekistan show the advances artisans made once they discovered glazing and firing. The cities were known by the colors of the domes of their buildings: blue in Samarqand, green in Khorezm, and gold in Bukhara.

Tall minarets with their tiled roofs are visible in many of the cities, where they glitter in the sun. Once they were used to call worshipers to prayer, but few minarets serve that function today. The entrances to the mosques are often richly decorated, tiled doorways that display the artistry and symbolism of Islam and its followers. The tiles covering the buildings were painted, carved or stamped.

Most of the rulers of Uzbekistan's city-states commissioned elaborate mausoleums, or mazars, sometimes to honor others but most often to improve their own reputations after death. These mausoleums still exist in the nation's cities, proof of the most advanced architectural techniques in use at the time and the lifework of thousands of artisans.

Most of the decoration on the mosques and the madrasas is floral or calligraphic (using stylized lettering), geometrically arranged around a central design. Although Islam forbids the artistic portrayal of animal life, the Central Asian artists were not as rigorously policed in that regard, and it is not unusual to find tigers, birds, or even the representations of people on holy structures. In Soviet days, the tile makers were commissioned to construct large murals that illustrated the cherished communist values of hard work and cooperation.

At the same time that architectural and building styles developed using the mud and natural dyes of the area, the craftsmen providing the markets with household utensils discovered the art of firing clay, which not only preserved their designs but strengthened their products. Today, potters throughout Uzbekistan still bring their colorful ceramic bowls, platters, and containers to the public markets to sell to tourists.

Much of the architecture in Uzbekistan features blue tiles with intricate patterns, such as those shown here.

UZBEK MUSIC

The music of Uzbekistan has much in common with other traditional Central Asian music. Persian as well as Azerbaijani and Uighur influences can be detected in the Uzbek sound. Uzbek classical music is called *shashmaqam*, and it dates to the 16th century in Bukhara. The word shashmaqam means "six modes." The six traditional modes are Rast, Nawa, Buzruk, Segah, Dugah, and Iraq. Like formal music throughout Central Asia, musical interludes alternate with spoken poetry. The music generally begins with low, quiet sounds that gradually rise in volume and pitch to a climactic peak before returning to the peaceful tones of the composition's opening section.

Traditional instruments include the *dutor*, a lute-like instrument with a long neck and two strings. The dutor has a warm, soothing tone and a history that can be traced to western China, where it was a shepherd's instrument, plucked and strummed to soothe the sheep. At the time of the Silk Road, the strings were woven from silk, but today they are generally made of nylon. The dombra, another long-necked, two-stringed instrument, resembles the mandolin and can be tapped, strummed, or plucked.

Typical Uzbek musical instruments are shown here.

The *doira* is a percussion instrument with similarities to both a drum and a tambourine. The musician holds the doira in their left hand, snapping at it with the fingers of the right. It can be very loud and is used as a solo instrument as well as part of an ensemble.

Another type of instrument is a flute called the *nai*. It is one of the world's oldest continuously played instruments, dating back around 5,000 years. The traditional nai is made of cane or reed, though modern nais are also made of metal, with five or six finger holes. The pitch can vary depending on the traditional demands of the music, but a master nai player can cover three octaves. Most orchestras have several nai players who can divide the range among them.

These are just a few of the instruments played throughout Uzbekistan. They are used to perform both classical music and the folk music heard in the streets and at every festival and wedding in the land. The musical traditions, spread by nomads and traders throughout Central Asia and beyond, have served as an aural record of the culture's vast creative output.

The tradition of playing music from other places continues in the nightclubs of the cities. There, talented young musicians supplement their traditional sounds with the computer-synthesized beats they borrow from European and North American performers. It is a sound their parents never heard growing up in Soviet isolation, and it is supplied mostly by the internet.

ILLUMINATED MANUSCRIPTS

The medieval miniature is a small intricate painting used to illustrate a book, or illuminated manuscript. It was an art form developed in Uzbekistan in the time of Tamerlane and is enjoying a revival in the Uzbek art world today. Often the renderings are made on papier-mâché. The medieval miniature was a crucial element in the books of the day. Most likely, the artists also used their skills to create boxes and other household items, but none of these survive today.

The painting style drew heavily from Chinese influences. In the manufacture of individual books, the artists illustrated not only the interior pages but also the leather bindings and covers that they decorated with intricate vines, flowers,

Illuminated manuscripts have small paintings that illustrate the book. Pages of an illuminated manuscript are shown here.

and elements from legends and classical literature. In the creation of books, the beauty of the calligraphy that set the words on the page was an essential element in determining the quality of the book. The colors found in surviving works help to determine their origin, since artists mixed their own paints and the chemical properties of the mud used in the mix differed from place to place.

The art of books was sometimes the art of politics as well. Often, stylized portraits of the person to whom the book was presented were incorporated into the text illustrations. The book might be about the family or the accomplishments of a particular ruler. The artists of today use many of the same techniques and symbols, which they alter and update slightly, giving a modern veneer to an ancient craft that often assumed political dimensions.

The most famous miniaturist was Behzad, born more than 550 years ago. His work brought historical personages to life and illustrated many classics of Asian poetry. His greatest accomplishment, besides having a superb technique, was the portrait miniature. Before him, the subjects of paintings were identifiable mainly by their dress, but his works faithfully and realistically reproduced the faces and figures of the people he was portraying.

FILM

Another art medium that is flourishing in Uzbekistan is film. UNESCO stated that the film industry is a promising cultural industry in Uzbekistan. In fact, the birthplace of film in Central Asia is Uzbekistan. The first film screening took place in Tashkent in 1897. In the 1920s, the first feature films in the region were created in Bukhara and Tashkent. In 2018, the Uzbekistan Film Commission was started by a decree by Mirziyoyev. The purpose of the commission is to increase tourism in Uzbekistan and to promote local film locations.

In 2019, the Centre for Contemporary Art opened in a former power station in Tashkent. The purpose of the center is to boost the undeveloped arts, such as film, experimental theatre, and choreography, in Uzbekistan. When the center opened, it featured an exhibit by Uzbek filmmaker Saodat Ismailova.

Ismailova has created art in a variety of mediums including video installations, multimedia performances, documentaries, and feature films. Her work *Qyrq Qyz*, produced by Aga Khan Music Initiative, is the story of 40 female warriors. The story is told through an all-women music group singing while playing traditional instruments in Karakalpakstan.

INTERNET LINKS

aspangallery.com/en/exhibition/www.aspangallery.com/eng/ornamentum
See examples of Dilyara Kaipova's work on the Aspan Gallery's exhibition page.

www.nytimes.com/2019/11/20/travel/tashkent-uzbekistan-subway.html
This *New York Times* article examines the history of Tashkent's subway art and includes many photos of the mosaics and chandeliers.

www.theguardian.com/artanddesign/2019/may/21/lost-louvre-uzbekistan-savitsky-museum-banned-art-stalin
Learn more about the museum that hid art that was banned by Stalin in this article on *The Guardian*'s website.

www.uzbekjourneys.com/2017/09/fantasy-world-of-uzbek-artist-Dilyara-Kaipova.html
Learn more about Dilyara Kaipova's work and see more examples of her work here.

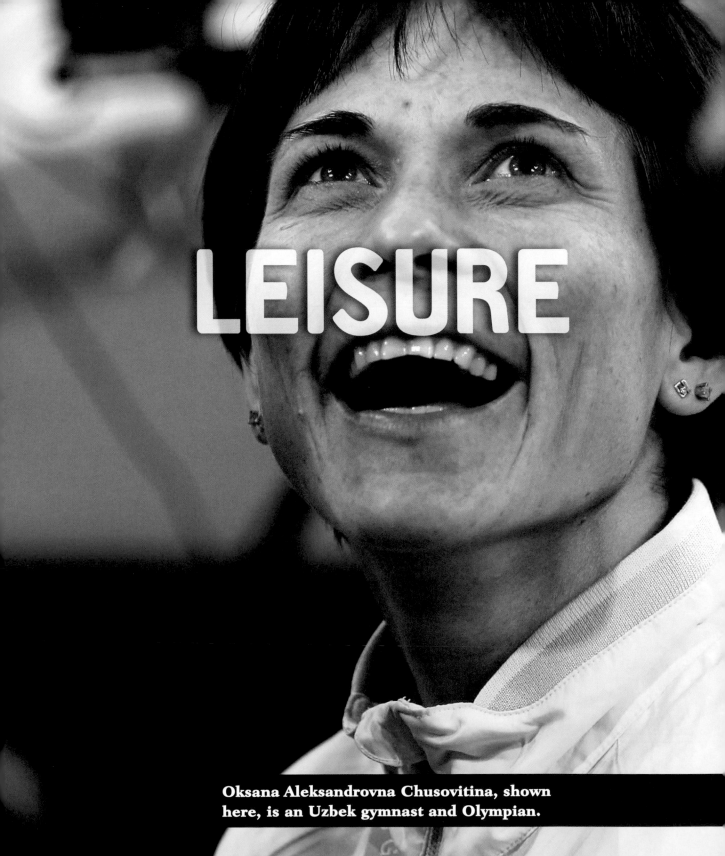

LEISURE

Oksana Aleksandrovna Chusovitina, shown here, is an Uzbek gymnast and Olympian.

11

RECREATIONAL ACTIVITIES OF THE people of Uzbekistan have deep cultural roots. Some of the games, such as football or rugby, may be familiar to people in other areas of the world. However, even those games that are played across different cultures have a deep meaning that reflects an aspect of Uzbek culture or has been adapted to suit their way of life.

THE GAME OF CHESS

The Soviets claimed that chess was invented in Uzbekistan. Though there is no consensus among experts about where exactly the game originated, most agree that it was spread along the Silk Road beginning in the second century CE. Uzbeks quickly adopted the game and have loved and played it ever since. In urban and village teahouses, men while away the hours drinking tea and perfecting their chess strategies, as they have for nearly 2,000 years. Children form clubs in schools to compete with others in chess leagues that sponsor matches throughout the country.

The State Museum of Samarqand houses the world's oldest-known chess pieces, which have been dated to 761 CE based on a coin found in the same layer at an archaeological site in Afrasiab, near Samarqand.

Uzbek men are shown here playing chess at a tea garden.

Uzbekistan has held a chess tournament most years since 1930.

There are seven pieces made of ivory: a chariot, two soldiers, an elephant, a horse, a king or queen, and a vizier (high-ranking court official or adviser).

Uzbekistan has a top chess master in Rustam Kasimdzhanov, born in 1979. Since childhood, Kasimdzhanov has been playing chess and competing internationally. He took second place in the Junior World Championship at the age of 18 and has participated in and won many international tournaments.

Uzbeks can play chess with a grandmaster on television. People mail in their moves, and the television station sends the most commonly received move to the grandmaster, who then makes a responding move. Each week, the show announces the moves, and the home viewers then are given the opportunity to contemplate their moves.

FOOTBALL

Football (called soccer in the United States) has been beloved since Soviet days. Like the other Soviet republics, Uzbekistan had its own team and competed in the Soviet leagues. Several of the Uzbek players were eventually promoted to the Soviet national team.

Uzbekistan's team was called Pakhtakor. It earned a permanent place in Uzbek history when, in 1979, a plane crash claimed the lives of the entire team. Every year, a match is played in memory of the Pakhtakor players.

Uzbekistan's football team is shown here in 2019.

When the Soviet Union dissolved, the Uzbek team became a member of the Asian Football League, where it competes in the yearly Asian Games. In 1994, it won the gold medal. The team now has its sights set on competing in the World Cup, the esteemed international championship held every four years.

Throughout the country, people eagerly follow their local teams and participate in a variety of school and semiprofessional leagues organized through their workplaces. Boys everywhere can be seen kicking footballs around the school yards and in the streets.

Women and girls play football in Uzbekistan too. Girls between ages 14 and 18 play competitively on teams, with the goal being a place on the national team. Occasionally, women and men play against each other.

BUZKASHI

Uzbeks play a form of polo that's familiar throughout Central Asia, though virtually unknown in the West. While the rules are similar, the equipment is not. Instead of a ball, Uzbeks use the carcass of a goat. Teams of riders on horseback demonstrate the skills that made ancient Asian horse soldiers feared by their enemies.

This polo game is known by many names. In Uzbekistan, it is most frequently called *kupkari* or *buzkashi*. Matches take place during the winter months and are often organized to coincide with weddings.

Teams of mounted riders battle fiercely over the dead body of a goat that has been weighted down with the addition of as much as 88 pounds (40 kg) of wet salt. The riders, armed with clubs and whips to subdue their competitors and spur their horses, fight for possession of the goat, which they deliver to the organizers of the match. A mounted referee oversees the match, which can last from noon to sundown.

Uzbekistan's Kumush Yuldashova (*right*) fights Mongolia's Otgon Munkhtsetseg (*left*) during a *kurash* event in 2018.

The riders often wear high leather boots, helmetlike fur hats, and padded jackets for protection, because attacking one another is a key part of the game. The boots' high heels are weapons that can be used as effectively as the whips and clubs. Horses are attacked as well as riders.

The match is made up of several rounds, each of which lasts between 15 and 30 minutes, or until the goat is delivered to the match organizers. The winners of each round receive prizes in the form of cash or cattle. The winners of the match at the end of the day can be awarded sheep, goats, camels, bulls, or even a car.

KURASH

Uzbeks wrestle in a vertical or upright style of jacketed fighting called *kurash*, which originated in Uzbekistan more than 3,500 years ago. Kurash—which means "grappling" in Uzbek—is believed, like many other Asian martial arts, to be a system of movement and combat that strengthens both mind and body. Tamerlane and his soldiers trained in kurash, and Uzbeks credit the sport with making his army unbeatable in its day. Perhaps as many as 2 million people participate in regular kurash matches and tournaments in Uzbekistan. Since independence, Uzbekistan has strongly promoted and organized international kurash meets, holding the first international tournament in Tashkent in 1998. Since then, international meets have been held in Turkey, South Africa, and Bolivia.

Kurash is promoted as a safe form of martial arts because it does not allow headlocks, choking, or strangling. Nor does it allow the players' knees to touch the ground or grappling below the waist. It is fast, dynamic, and fun to watch. Throughout Uzbekistan, boys watch competitions with their fathers and practice with their friends.

The style of wrestling that occurs on a mat or on the ground, with which North Americans are most commonly familiar, is also practiced in Uzbekistan. Wrestlers were given a special incentive when they competed in the 2004 Olympic Games in Athens, Greece: money. The government rewarded gold medal winners with $100,000; silver medal winners with $50,000; and bronze medal winners with $25,000. To the delight of everyone, Uzbekistan's wrestlers triumphed, returning home with two gold medals and one silver medal.

Theater and music are celebrated in Uzbekistan. The Hamza Theatre in Tashkent is shown here.

PERFORMING ARTS

Theater and music have always been celebrated in Uzbekistan. Wealthy rulers served as patrons of theater and ballet companies to spread the glory of their own names. Soviet programs to train performers and maintain national theater, ballet, and opera companies continued under Karimov. The folk tradition also lives on in performances at every festival and wedding held throughout the country. Uzbeks rightly take for granted that performances are inexpensive or free and are theirs to enjoy. Even during the present days of economic hardship, the performing arts are alive and flourishing, fostered by both the government and family traditions.

In the cities, especially in Tashkent, there are several theaters and concert halls. The return of interest in Uzbek culture since independence has led to the development of ballet, opera, and theater companies that perform the works of contemporary Uzbek writers and composers as well as the classic works of many cultures. The Youth Theatre of Uzbekistan and the Puppet Theater were established under the Soviets and thrive today, giving performances for Uzbekistani children during regular seasons and appearing throughout the country at festivals.

RUGBY

Rugby is played with an oval ball and consists of two teams of 13 players (rugby league play) or 15 players (rugby union play). Both play types originate from the style of football that was played at the Rugby School in England. The fact that rugby is played in Uzbekistan reflects the changing political nature of the country. Rugby was played in Russia prior to the 1917 revolution; however, it was banned during Soviet rule. After Stalin died in 1953, it was reintroduced and gained a following in Uzbekistan. In 1962, four teams were founded. In 2002, the Uzbekistan Rugby Federation (URF) was founded.

UZBEKISTAN SPECIAL OLYMPICS

The Special Olympics are a global organization for athletes with disabilities. Every year, these athletes work with volunteers and coaches to prepare for the games. There are periodic events throughout the year for the Special Olympics, and the organization also provides year-round sports training that is important for people with disabilities. In addition to training, the athletes also get the added benefits of friendship, joy, and the learning of new skills.

The Uzbekistan division was founded in 2001, and as of 2020, there are more than 21,000 athletes. Gulya Saidova, who is the vice president of Special Olympics Uzbekistan, has the goal of bringing in even more participants with disabilities who have never participated in sports. Getting children with disabilities involved in organizations such as this helps to break the stigma, or negative opinions, against people with disabilities. Overall, it also helps families and communities to see people with disabilities and help to normalize these differences.

Rugby is not limited to men—since 2008, the women's team has competed in international tournaments.

As of 2020, the national rugby team has not yet played in a World Cup. Rugby is still a minority sport in Uzbekistan; however, it is attracting a growing number of fans as well as players.

INTERNET LINKS

www.uzbekembassy.in/on-the-history-of-appearance-of-chess-in-the-territory-of-modern-uzbekistan/
This page examines the history of chess in Uzbekistan.

uzbek.org.uk/sports-in-uzbekistan/
This page includes information about sports in Uzbekistan.

FESTIVALS

A woman in a traditional costume celebrates Nowruz in Tashkent.

12

ESTIVALS ARE AN IMPORTANT PART of the Uzbek culture. They're often official holidays, a state of mind, and a celebration. In addition to national holidays such as Nowruz, there are vibrant smaller festivals that can be found outside of the large cities. One of these is the Boysun Bahori festival, which is celebrated in a small city in southern Uzbekistan.

NESCO named the Boysun culture a Masterpiece of Oral and Intangible Cultural Heritage in 2001.

NOWRUZ FESTIVAL

March 21 marks the beginning of the new year and the first day of spring in Uzbekistan, and it's commonly considered the universal day for celebrations of renewal and rebirth. In Uzbekistan, it is called Nowruz, a word composed of two Uzbek words—*now*, meaning "new," and *ruz*, meaning "day." Unlike in the West, where New Year's Eve is celebrated with parties or lively social events, Nowruz is a daytime festival, spent with one's family close to home.

The two-day festival of Nowruz has been celebrated for at least 2,500 years. It originated in Persia, where legend has it that Jamshid, a Persian king from mythology, was carried in a chariot through the air. This accomplishment amazed his subjects, and they had a festival that same day. Nomads moving into the Persian lands of Central Asia adopted this rite of spring, following the course of the moon to set the dates of their celebrations as well as their migrations and plantings. Though they did not refer to calendars, people knew this was the time when the days lengthened and warmed, and the growing season began again. People who settled in oasis towns and villages held street fairs and athletic competitions. Wandering minstrels called *baxshi* recited epic poems and sang, women prepared their most festive foods, and town parks and village squares were filled with music and dancing. To this day, despite thousands of years of change and many foreign occupations, when March 21 comes around each year, Nowruz is celebrated in much the same way.

The traditional Uzbek meal for Nowruz is called *sumalyak*. Over an open wood fire, women slowly cook the sumalyak, a cereal dish made of flour, spices, and sprouted grains of wheat. Sprouted wheat has ancient meaning as it symbolizes life and plenty. Tajiks in Uzbekistan have stronger ties to Persia, and their Nowruz meal reflects this particular influence. In Tajik families, the men and sons prepare the meal of shish kebabs and sweetened rice in hopes of sweetening the future. Elders bestow their blessings on children and give them gifts, making Nowruz the favorite holiday for young people throughout the country.

Dancers are shown here at a Nowruz festival in Tashkent.

- *Independence Day (Mustakillik Bayrami) is celebrated on September 1. This holiday commemorates when Uzbekistan declared independence from the Soviet Union, which actually took place August 31. Fireworks, competitions, and concerts are included in the celebrations held on this day.*

- *Flag Day is held on November 18 and is a solemn day for citizens. On this day in 1991, the state flag was legalized. The previous flag had ties to communism with red-blue-red stripes.*

- *Constitution Day is observed on December 8. It is a celebration of the day that the constitution of Uzbekistan was adopted in 1992.*

Central Asia is the land of the horse, and in Uzbekistan, Nowruz is a day for horse races. There are also concerts, drama festivals, trade shows, and wrestling matches. However, it is a time for personal renewal as well. People prepare for the new year by cleaning their homes, buying and making new clothes, canceling debts, forgiving slights, and generally turning a new face to the future. They welcome the onset of the growing season by filling their homes with the fragrant branches of flowering fruit and nut trees, including almond, apricot, peach, and pomegranate. All these household preparations are completed before the morning star appears March 21. The celebration of spring can then continue over the next two weeks, as Uzbeks move outdoors for gatherings of family and friends. They start the new growing season by setting out seedlings and planting new trees.

EASTER

Around 9 percent of Uzbeks are Eastern Orthodox Christians, and, for them, the celebration of Easter is a welcome sign of spring whenever it occurs. Like Islamic holidays, the date varies from year to year. Even though there is a very small population of Eastern Orthodox Christians, Easter is celebrated and recognized by vendors throughout the country. Vendors sell painted eggs; *kulich*, which is a type of sweetened Easter bread; and other candies and sweet treats.

RELIGIOUS HOLIDAYS

Islamic holidays vary by date according to the phases of the moon. The nation's president issues a decree each year establishing the dates of the upcoming holidays.

One Islamic holiday is Eid al-Adha—the Feast of Sacrifice. Religious rituals and prayers begin this special observance as they do all days. Eid al-Adha, or Kurban-Hayit, as it is called in Uzbekistan, is particularly significant for people who are making the journey to Mecca.

Eid al-Fitr celebrates the end of Ramadan, the month of contemplation and fasting. To mark the observance, people begin their day with prayers of thanksgiving and devotion. They bathe and dress in their best clothes. Children receive gifts, and friends and families celebrate together with feasting and traditional music and dance. On this day above all others, people are urged to remember the poor with gifts and to visit the sick and elderly as well. In Uzbekistan, this holiday is called Ramadan-Hayit.

NONRELIGIOUS CELEBRATIONS

Uzbeks celebrate other holidays as well. Like people in the West, they give cards and candy on February 14, Valentine's Day. April 1 is known as April Fool's Day and is marked by people trying to trick one another with silly jokes and pranks.

January 14 is the Day of Motherland Defenders, which is celebrated with parades and fireworks. On this day, military men dress in full uniform and line up to accept awards and congratulations.

March 8 is International Women's Day, which is celebrated worldwide. During this day in Uzbekistan, men honor the women in their lives and celebrate them with flowers and gifts. On this day, women gather at a concert hall called Istiklol Palace to hear music or to celebrate female participation in historical events.

Besides the Day of Motherland Defenders and International Women's Day, the government observes a Day of Memory and Honor on May 9 with a military parade that pays tribute to the veterans of World War II. September 1 is Independence Day, commemorating Uzbekistan's independence from the Soviet Union and the declaration of its sovereignty. On November 18, street festivals are held to honor the state flag, and on December 8, street festivals are held to celebrate the nation's post-independence constitution.

BOYSUN BAHORI FESTIVAL

The Boysun Bahori festival was first celebrated in 2002, the year after UNESCO named Boysun a Masterpiece of Oral and Intangible Cultural Heritage. Boysun is one unique place in Uzbekistan that has preserved Uzbek traditions and continues to practice them in everyday life. The festival celebrates traditional Uzbek culture and is held in the spring, when the mountains surrounding Boysun are covered with flowers and foliage. A yurt camp is set up, and the festival includes workshops, stages for folk ensembles, and arenas for kurash and other competitions.

INTERNET LINKS

en.unesco.org/silkroad/content/nowruz-celebrating-new-year-silk-roads
This in-depth article provides a history of the Nowruz festival and how it is celebrated.

ich.unesco.org/en/RL/cultural-space-of-boysun-district-00019
This page on UNESCO's website is about the Boysun district and festivals.

FOOD

Fruits and vegetables are plentiful in markets
in Uzbekistan such as the one shown here.

13

Uzbekistan's food shares a close resemblance to dishes from Turkey and China, as well as other Eastern Asian cuisines.

UZBEK CUISINE CONSISTS OF RICH, hearty food. Many of the dishes also have a lot of calories. The purpose of this is to provide workers in the fields with enough sustenance to get them through the day. Staple ingredients include rice, flour, vegetables, oil, and meat that comes primarily from sheep. Spices such as cinnamon, bay leaves, coriander, and cumin are also prominent in the cuisine.

FRESH PRODUCE

In summer, Uzbekistan's markets and kitchens are filled with fruits and vegetables grown in the Fergana Valley. Grapes, apricots, pears, apples, cherries, and citrus fruits find their way into desserts and wines.

Peaches from Uzbekistan once drew the interest of the Chinese and heightened their curiosity about their Uzbek neighbors to the west. The pomegranate with its brilliant red seeds is also important to the cuisine. Traditionally, women dried summer fruits so they could have them for winter.

Figs, apricots, raisins, and dates still add their sweetness to winter stews and desserts.

Besides the fruits of summer, Uzbekistan grows a wide variety of vegetables. Some are familiar to people everywhere: onions, eggplants, and cucumbers, as well as root vegetables. Others are varieties of familiar vegetables available only in Central Asia, such as yellow carrots and green radishes. Many cooks have unique family recipes for the wide array of pumpkins and squashes that appear in the markets throughout the long growing season.

MEAT

Meat is not plentiful in Uzbekistan. It is generally combined with rice and vegetables to make it go further. The fat-tailed Karakul sheep that provides the wool for rugs and other textiles also provides the most commonly available meat and fat. Beef and horsemeat can be substituted for mutton (older sheep) in most recipes. Two types of sausage are unique to the region: *piyozli kazy*, or horsemeat sausages, and *khassip*, a sausage made of sheep's intestines and lungs.

SPICES

As a country that is at the crossroads of trade with the East, Uzbekistan has many spices such as cumin and pepper that feature prominently in many dishes. The leaves of one plant provide a common herb, cilantro, but its dried seeds provide a totally different taste in the form of coriander. Uzbek cooks use plenty of both. Parsley, dill, and basil are commonly found both in the markets and growing in small home herb gardens.

TEA AND TEA CEREMONIES

Tea and the ceremonies that surround the making and drinking of it are central to Uzbek life. Throughout the country in cities and villages, men gather daily at the teahouse (*choyxona*) to drink green tea and talk.

The choyxona itself is constructed according to regional traditions. It is built in the shade of a wooded area, often near a water source. The walls are open to catch the breezes, and patrons sit on low stools or recline on a raised platform called a *supa*. People remove their shoes before entering the choyxona and sit with their legs stretched out under the low table or curled beneath them

Uzbekistan has a wide variety of rich, hearty foods. The recipes generally vary between regions of the country. However, there are certain recipes that are national dishes. These recipes are widely available and commonly eaten throughout Uzbekistan. They include:

- plov, *which is a type of rice pilaf made with meat, carrots, and rice.*
- non, *which is a traditional bread that is cooked in a* tandyr *(clay oven).*
- somsa, *which is meat- and onion-filled pastry.*
- lagman, *which is a soup made with noodles and meat.*
- manti, *which are steamed meat- and onion-filled dumplings.*
- naryn, *which is made with meat and handmade noodles.*
- shurpa, *which is a meat and vegetable soup.*
- shashlik, *which are skewers of grilled meats with spices.*

on the supa. The guests sit where the host directs them. The farther they are seated from the door, the greater the honor bestowed on them.

In homes or choyxonas, the tea ceremony is the same. The host pours tea three times into their cup, which is called a piala, each time pouring it back into the pot. This further steeps the tea leaves, making the tea more flavorful. Then, the host pours the brew for their guests, serving them one at a time. As each guest takes the piala from the host, they salute one another by placing their left hands on their hearts. The guest says *rahmat*, or "thank you."

Tea is central to the pace of Uzbek life. A hot climate does not reward those who hurry, so life proceeds in Uzbekistan at a leisurely pace. Tea helps set the pace with its almost ritualized preparation. Brewing it, waiting for it to cool, and drinking it all take time, and Uzbeks take many tea breaks. The common answer to a question about when something will happen is "after tea." It is not unusual for the answer to be "tea after tea," which is clearly understood by all to mean, "not in the very near future."

The choyxona is also a place where there are no class divisions. Whether scientist or truck driver, janitor or doctor, when Uzbeks take tea together, they show interest in and respect for one another with no regard for rank or status. Increasing unemployment has made the choyxona the only destination for many men. They gather there to commiserate with those who are often facing similarly challenging economic realities.

INTEREST IN UZBEK FOOD

Plov is the most famous dish of Uzbekistan. According to legend, the dish first came to be around the time of Tamerlane. He needed to feed his large armies, so this dish of rice, carrots, and meat was determined to be the ideal food because it was both easily transported and high in calories. Plov is eaten at almost every special occasion in Uzbekistan, and it is also eaten nearly daily outside of those occasions. However, some researchers are wondering if too much plov is a bad thing. The problem with this dish is the high-calorie oil that features heavily in the recipe. According to a 2017 study, Uzbekistan had the highest number of diet-related deaths—892 per 100,000 people a year. In the study, a poor diet consisted of too much salt, too few fruits and

A food stall at the Tashkent market is shown here.

vegetables, and not enough whole grains. However, Lola Abdurakhimova, a gastroenterologist from Uzbekistan, argues that the issue is not the food itself, but rather lifestyle changes including overeating and sedentary routines in which people are not moving around a lot. Abdurakhimova also stated that there is a lack of fruits and vegetables in the typical Uzbek diet. Whereas fruits and vegetables used to be snacks, now they are replaced with hamburgers and other foreign fast foods.

However, while foreign fast food has had an impact on Uzbek cuisine, Uzbek cuisine is also starting to have an impact on the rest of the world. Since Mirziyoyev has instituted reforms and opened up the country more, tourism is also increasing. In 2018, food vlogger Mark Wiens did a food tour of Uzbekistan, and his videos were watched more than 10 million times. People are becoming increasingly interested in the food of Uzbekistan, priming it to make an impact on cuisine in the rest of the world.

INTERNET LINKS

www.bbc.com/travel/gallery/20191117-is-uzbek-cuisine-actually-to-die-for
This article on the BBC Travel website includes photos and information about Uzbek cuisine.

www.latimes.com/archives/la-xpm-1992-06-25-fo-1443-story.html
This *LA Times* article has information about Uzbek food and includes some recipes.

SOMSAS

Filling:

1 ½ pounds (0.68 kilograms) chicken
  thighs or breast

2 potatoes, finely cubed

½ large onion, finely chopped

1 garlic clove, minced

2 tablespoons cold butter, grated

¼ teaspoon ground cumin

½ teaspoon ground coriander

½ teaspoon salt

¼ teaspoon ground black pepper

2 teaspoons mayonnaise

Topping:

4 tablespoons melted butter

1 tablespoon sesame seeds

16 ounces (0.45 kg) phyllo dough

Preheat the oven to 400°F, and line two large baking sheets with parchment paper. Combine the spices in a bowl, and set aside. Cut the chicken into small cubes, and finely chop the onion, mince the garlic, and finely cube the potatoes. Combine the chicken, onions, garlic, potatoes, spices, mayonnaise, and grated butter into a bowl, and stir to combine. Next, unwrap and unroll the phyllo dough and take four sheets of the dough. Place one sheet onto your working surface, and lightly brush it with some of the melted butter. Continue this for all four sheets. Cut the sheets in half lengthwise with a pizza cutter to create two equal parts. Next, add a generous spoonful of the filling to the corner end of each rectangle, leaving room around the filling. Fold the other corner over the filling to create a triangle, and press down on the edges to seal the filling into your pastry. Continue with the remaining ingredients. Brush the tops of each pastry with melted butter, and sprinkle with the sesame seeds. Place the pastries onto your prepared baking sheet, and top with foil. Bake for 18 minutes, remove foil, then bake for an additional 10 to 12 minutes. This recipe makes 18 pastries.

SHASHLIK

This recipe makes about 4 cups (approximately 4 servings).

Marinade:

¼ cup (59 milliliters) distilled
   white vinegar
1 tablespoon canola oil
1 large yellow onion, thinly sliced
2 bay leaves, crumbled
1 teaspoon cumin seeds
½ teaspoon ground cumin
½ teaspoon coriander seeds
   (optional)
½ teaspoon black peppercorns
6 allspice berries
salt
pepper

Meat:

2 lamb leg steaks, 1 to 1 ¼ inches (2.54 to 3.2 centimeters) thick, cut into 1 ¼-inch (3.2 cm)
   pieces

Combine the marinade ingredients in a sealable gallon bag, and shake or squeeze to combine. Add the lamb steak cubes to the bag, and turn to coat. Seal the bag again, letting out all the air. Marinate overnight in the refrigerator. When ready to cook, set the bag out at room temperature for about half an hour. Next, remove the lamb from the marinade, and pat dry with paper towels. Remove any bits of spices and onions that are sticking to the meat. Stick the meat onto skewers (either soaked bamboo or metal skewers), and grill for 10 to 14 minutes. Serve with flatbread or rice.

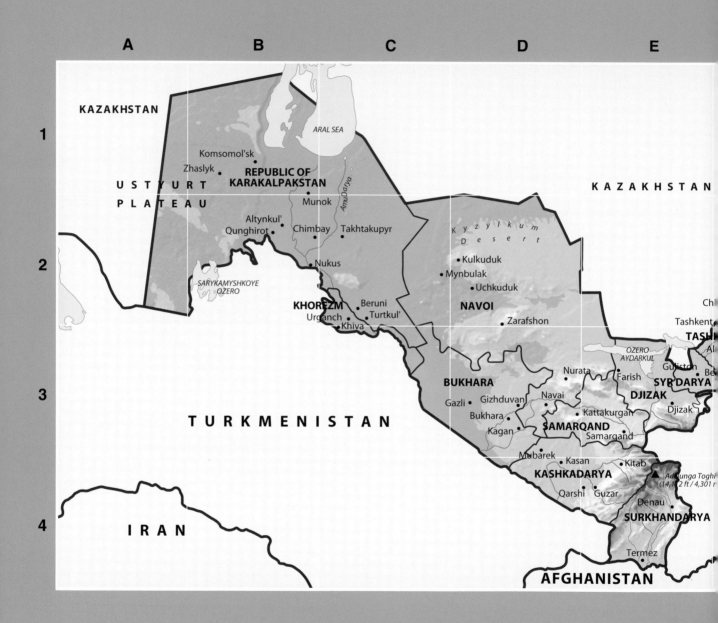

MAP OF UZBEKISTAN

F   **G**

- ● Capital city
- ● Major town
- ▲ Mountain peak

Feet	Meters
9,900	3,000
6,600	2,000
3,300	1,000
1,650	500
660	200
0	0

Gora Manas
(14,705 ft / 4,482 m)

KYRGYZSTAN

Namangan

Angren

NAMANGAN

Andizhan

ANDIZHAN

Kokand

FERGANA

Fergana

CHINA

TAJIKISTAN

PAKISTAN

Adelunga Toghi, E4
Almalyk, F3
Altynkul', B2
Amu Darya, B2, C1, C2, C3
Andizhan, G3
Angren, F3
Aral Sea, B1, C1

Bekabad, F3
Beruni, C2
Bukhara, D3

Chimbay, B2
Chirchik, F2

Denau, E4
Djizak, E3

Farish, E3
Fergana, F3

Gazli, D3,
Gizhduvan, D3
Gora Manas, F2
Guliston, E3
Guzar, E4

Kagan, D3
Kasan, D4
Kattakurgan, D3
Khiva, C2
Kitab, E4
Kokand, F3
Komsomol'sk, B1

Kulkuduk, D2
Kyzyl Kum Desert, D2, E2

Mubarek, D3
Munok, B1
Mynbulak, C2

Namangan, F3
Navoi, D3
Nukus, B2
Nurata, D3

Ozero Aydarkul, E3

Qarshi, E4
Qunghirot, B2

Samarqand, E3
Sarykamyshkoye Ozero, B2

Takhtakupyr, C2
Tashkent, F2
Termez, E4
Turtkul', C2

Uchkuduk, D2
Urganch, C2

Zarafshon, D2
Zhaslyk, B1

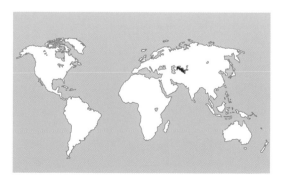

ECONOMIC UZBEKISTAN

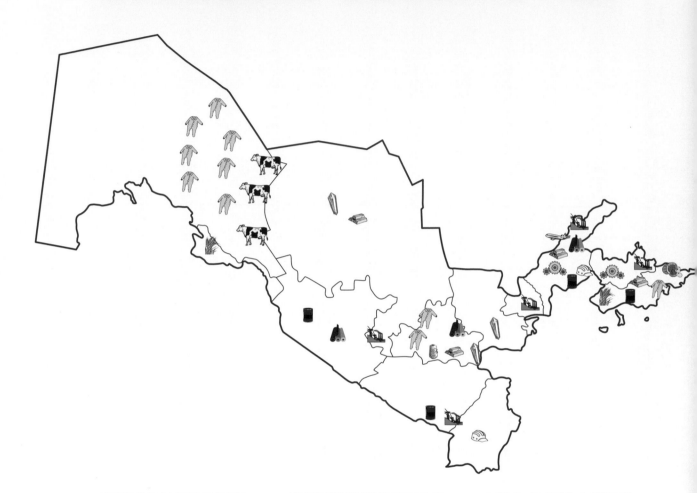

 Agriculture

 Alfalfa

 Cotton

 Fruit

 Livestock

 Silk

Natural Resources

 Coal

 Gold

 Oil and Natural Gas

 Uranium

Manufacturing

 Machinery

 Textiles

Services

 Airport

 Power Station

ABOUT THE ECONOMY

All figures are 2017 estimates unless otherwise noted.

GROSS DOMESTIC PRODUCT (GDP)
$48.83 billion

PER CAPITA GDP
$6,900

GDP BY SECTOR
agriculture 17.9 percent, industry 33.7 percent, services 48.5 percent

GDP REAL GROWTH RATE
5.3 percent

LAND AREA
172,742 square miles (447,400 sq km)

LAND USE
arable land 10.1 percent, permanent crops 0.8 percent, other 51.7 percent

NATURAL RESOURCES
gold, natural gas, petroleum, coal, silver, copper, uranium, lead and zinc, tungsten, molybdenum

INFLATION RATE
12.5 percent

CURRENCY
Uzbekistani sum (UZS)
USD (U.S. dollar) 1 = UZS 3,906.1

INDUSTRIES
textiles, food processing, metallurgy, machine building, mining, chemicals, hydrocarbon extraction

MAIN EXPORTS
cotton, gold, energy products, mineral fertilizers, metals

IMPORTS
machinery, food, chemicals, metals

EXPORTS
$11.48 billion

TRADE PARTNERS
Switzerland, China, Russia, Kazakhstan, Turkey, Afghanistan, South Korea, Germany

WORKFORCE
18.2 million

WORKFORCE BY OCCUPATION
agriculture 25.9 percent; industry 13.2 percent; services, including military, 60.9 percent

UNEMPLOYMENT RATE
5 percent

POVERTY RATE
14 percent

EXTERNAL DEBT
$16.9 billion

CULTURAL UZBEKISTAN

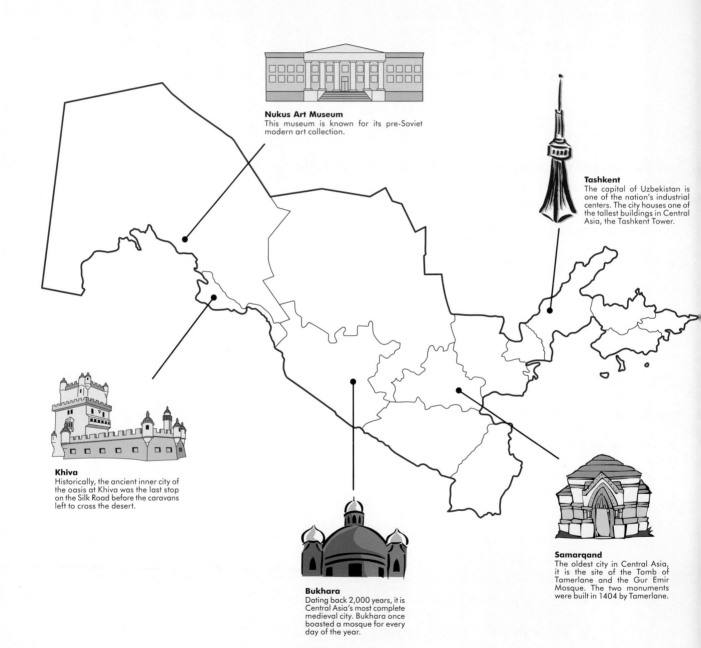

Nukus Art Museum
This museum is known for its pre-Soviet modern art collection.

Tashkent
The capital of Uzbekistan is one of the nation's industrial centers. The city houses one of the tallest buildings in Central Asia, the Tashkent Tower.

Khiva
Historically, the ancient inner city of the oasis at Khiva was the last stop on the Silk Road before the caravans left to cross the desert.

Bukhara
Dating back 2,000 years, it is Central Asia's most complete medieval city. Bukhara once boasted a mosque for every day of the year.

Samarqand
The oldest city in Central Asia, it is the site of the Tomb of Tamerlane and the Gur Emir Mosque. The two monuments were built in 1404 by Tamerlane.

ABOUT THE CULTURE

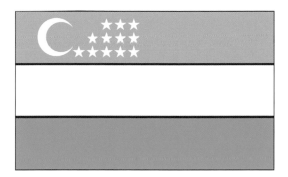

All figures are 2017 estimates unless otherwise noted.

OFFICIAL NAME
Republic of Uzbekistan

CAPITAL
Tashkent

OTHER MAJOR CITIES
Samarqand, Bukhara

GOVERNMENT SYSTEM
presidential republic, highly authoritarian

FLAG
three equal horizontal bands of blue (top), white (middle), and green separated by red fimbriations with a white crescent moon and 12 white stars in the upper hoist-side quadrant

NATIONAL ANTHEM
O'zbekiston Respublikasining Davlat Madhiyasi

POPULATION
30,565,411 (July 2020)

POPULATION GROWTH RATE
1.7 percent (2019)

POPULATION DENSITY
186.87 per square mile (72.02 per sq km)

LIFE EXPECTANCY
74.8 years

LITERACY RATE
100 percent

ETHNIC GROUPS
Uzbek 83.8 percent, Tajik 4.8 percent, Kazakh 2.5 percent, Russian 2.3 percent, Karakalpak 2.2 percent, Tatar 1.5 percent, other 4.4 percent

MAJOR RELIGIONS
Muslim 88 percent (mostly Sunnis), Eastern Orthodox 9 percent, others 3 percent

OFFICIAL LANGUAGE
Uzbek

NATIONAL HOLIDAY
September 1

LEADERS IN POLITICS
Achilbay Ramatov (first deputy prime minister/minister of transport since 2016), Abdulla Aripov (prime minister since 2016), Shavkat Mirziyoyev (president since 2016)

LEADERS IN THE ARTS
Zakirjan Furqat (poet), Pavel Benkov (painter), Abdullah Oripov (poet)

TIMELINE

IN UZBEKISTAN	IN THE WORLD
100 BCE Samarqand, Bukhara, and Khiva are important cities on the Silk Road.	
CE 700 Islam is established in Central Asia.	
900 Persian dynasty rules the Central Asian region with Bukhara as its center.	**117** The Roman Empire reaches its greatest extent, under Emperor Trajan (98–117).
	1530 The beginning of the transatlantic slave trade is organized by the Portuguese in Africa.
	1620 The Pilgrims sail the *Mayflower* to America.
	1775–1783 The American Revolution is fought.
	1776 The U.S. Declaration of Independence is written.
	1789–1799 The French Revolution takes place.
1865 Russians seize control of Tashkent and from there rule much of Central Asia, though not all of Uzbekistan.	**1861** The American Civil War begins.
1881 The Battle at Geok-Tepe gives control of all of Uzbekistan to czarist Russia.	
	1914 World War I begins.
1917 The Bolshevik revolution in Russia establishes communism in Tashkent.	**1918** Fighting in World War I ends.
1924 The Uzbek Soviet Socialist Republic is formed and becomes part of the Soviet Union.	**1939** World War II begins.

IN UZBEKISTAN	IN THE WORLD
1930s–1940s	**1945**
Ethnic minorities and dissidents are deported, resettled, or murdered.	The United States drops atomic bombs on Hiroshima and Nagasaki at the end of World War II.
1950s–1980s	**1957**
Irrigation makes cotton Uzbekistan's main crop and begins the devastation of the Aral Sea.	The Russians launch *Sputnik*.
	1986
	A nuclear power disaster occurs at Chernobyl in Ukraine.
1989	
Islam Karimov is named head of the Uzbek Communist Party.	
1991	**1991**
Uzbekistan becomes independent.	The Soviet Union breaks up.
1992	
Opposition parties are banned.	
1995	
Dissidents are sentenced to long prison terms.	**2001**
	Terrorists crash planes in New York, Washington, D.C., and Pennsylvania on September 11.
	2003
2004–2005	The Iraq War begins.
Trade and religious restrictions lead to protests. The government retaliates with force.	**2008**
	Barack Obama is elected the first African American president of the United States.
2016	
Shavkat Mirziyoyev comes to power as president after the death of Karimov.	
2019	
Tanzila Narbaeva becomes the first female speaker of the senate.	**2020**
	COVID-19 spreads quickly across the world and is declared a pandemic. Additionally, the murder of George Floyd results in worldwide protests as a part of the Black Lives Matter movement.

GLOSSARY

abrbandchi
The artisan who applies the pattern of the warp while making silk.

baxshi
Wandering minstrels and poets who enlivened festivals in former days.

choyxona
A traditional teahouse.

doira
A percussion instrument.

dombra
A two-stringed musical instrument shaped like a mandolin.

dutor
A two-stringed musical instrument that is plucked and strummed by the musician.

gul
An eight-sided design characteristic of Central Asian weaving and architecture.

hokim
A governor.

kolkhoz
A large collective farm made up of small farms that were seized and run by the Soviet government.

mustakillik
Independence.

nai
A kind of flute.

non
Uzbek bread.

plov
A rice-and-lamb dish, with other ingredients added according to tradition and the cook's preference.

shashlik
A dish prepared by men; mutton grilled on a stick, similar to a gyro.

shashmaqam
Classical Uzbek music.

sumalyak
A traditional dish for the celebration of spring.

suzani
A type of fabric.

tubeteika
A type of skull-cap that men and women wear.

viloyat
A province.

vizier
Historically, a high-ranking official or adviser in a Muslim kingdom.

yurt
The nomad's mobile home, a house-sized tent made of felted wool over a lattice frame.

FOR FURTHER INFORMATION

BOOKS

Alexander, Christopher Aslan. *A Carpet Ride to Khiva: Seven Years on the Silk Road*. London, UK: Icon Books, 2010.

Fatland, Erica. *Sovietstan: Travels in Turkmenistan, Kazakhstan, Tajikistan, Kyrgyztstan, and Uzbekistan*. New York, NY: Pegasus Books, 2020.

Libal, Joyce. *Uzbekistan: The Growth and Influence of Islam in the Nations of Asia and Central Asia*. Broomall, PA: Mason Crest Publishers, 2005.

MacLeod, Calum. *Uzbekistan: The Golden Road to Samarkand*. Hong Kong, China: Odyssey Books & Maps, 2014.

McCray, Thomas R. *Uzbekistan (Modern World Nations)*. Broomall, PA: Chelsea House, 2004.

Ulko, Alex. *Uzbekistan — Culture Smart!: The Essential Guide to Customs & Culture*. London, UK: Kuperard, 2017.

Wilson, Paul. *The Silk Roads: Includes Turkey, Syria, Iran, Turkmenistan, Uzbekistan, Kyrgyzstan, Kazakhstan, Pakistan and China*. London, UK: Trailblazer Publications, 2007.

WEBSITES

Embassy of Uzbekistan in Washington, D.C. www.uzbekistan.org.

Human Rights Watch: Uzbekistan. www.hrw.org/europe/central-asia/uzbekistan.

The SilkRoad Project Website. www.silkroad.org.

The New Humanitarian. www.irinnews.org/AsiaFp.asp?SelectRegion=Asia&SelectCountry= Uzbekistan.

Permanent Mission of the Republic of Uzbekistan to the UN Office and other International Organisations in Geneva. uzbekistan-geneva.ch.

Uzbek Government Web Portal. www.gov.uz.

VIDEOS

Central Asia: Kyrgyzstan and Uzbekistan. Lonely Planet, 1997.

MUSIC

Music of Uzbekistan: Hidden Central Asian Treasure. Smithsonian Folkways, 1991.

Music of Uzbekistan. Tanbur, 2013.

National Folk Music Orchestra of Uzbekistan. *Music of Uzbekistan*. Arc Music, 2003.

BIBLIOGRAPHY

Chen, Dene-Hern. "The Country That Brought a Sea Back to Life." *BBC*, July 23, 2018. www.bbc. com/future/article/20180719-how-kazakhstan-brought-the-aral-sea-back-to-life.

CIA. *The World Factbook*. "Uzbekistan." www.cia.gov/library/publications/the-world-factbook/ geos/uz.html.

"Country Facts." The Permanent Mission of the Republic of Uzbekistan to the United Nations. www.un.int/uzbekistan/uzbekistan/country-facts.

Howell, Elizabeth. "The Aral Sea Drying Out. This NASA Time-Lapse Video Shows It from Space." Space.com, May 8, 2019. www.space.com/aral-sea-dries-up-time-lapse.html.

Nurullayev, Dmitriy. "Uzbekistan's Succession Question Is Russia's Strategic Opportunity." *The Diplomat*, September 4, 2016. thediplomat.com/2016/09/uzbekistans-succession-question-is-russias-strategic-opportunity/.

Olmos, Francisco. "The Curious Case of the Republic of Karakalpakstan." The Foreign Policy Centre, May 28, 2020. fpc.org.uk/the-curious-case-of-the-republic-of-karakalpakstan/.

Ramachandra, Komala. "Forced Labor Persists in Uzbekistan's Cotton Fields." Human Rights Watch, June 25, 2020. www.hrw.org/news/2020/06/25/forced-labor-persists-uzbekistans-cotton-fields.

Smith, David Roger. "Uzbekistan." *Encyclopedia Britannica*, March 27, 2020. www.britannica. com/place/Uzbekistan.

"Uzbek Lamb Kebabs and Marinades Updates." Hungry Cravings, June 11, 2014. www. hungrycravings.com/2014/06/uzbek-lamb-kebabs-and-marinades-updates.html.

"Uzbek Samosa Recipe." Valentina's Corner, September 18, 2018. valentinascorner.com/uzbek-samsa-recipe/.

INDEX

INDEX